Entrepreneurship Success Handbook

TABLE OF CONTENTS

COPYRIGHT
Chapter 1:
Go for the Gold
  Be Confident
  Be a Machine
  Be Charitable
  Be a Success
  Be There and Be Aware
  Be the Edge
Chapter 2:
Make a Winning Plan
  Plan Your Success in Writing
  Quit Your Job
  Get Incorporated and Situated
  The Naming Process
  Logos and Slogans
  Make Progress
Chapter 3:
Best Practices as Weapons
  Don't Deny Better Opportunities
  Do Zero-Based Budgeting of the Mind
  Get First Mover Advantage
  Embrace Natural Selection
  Welcome to Hype Theory
  Gain Consensus
  Master Efficiency, Leverage, and Scale
  Oh, Oh, Domino

   Sell Your Company
   Kaizen: A Japanese Way to Approach Best Practices
   Best Practices for Your Team

Chapter 4:
Modern Methods of Business Domination
   Globalization
   Communicating Today
   Keeping Your Word
   Co-opetition
   Use Data Wisely
   Reporting and Documentation
   Control Intellectual Property
   Get It in (Simple) Writing
   Harness Internet Power
   The Future of the Internet and Technology
   What are Domain Names & Why Do I Need Some?
   The Importance of SEO
   Finding What You Need Online

Chapter 5:
Make Dollars Use Sense
   Hedge Risk
   But be Decisive while Hedging
   Purchasing Strategy
   Price it Right
   Negotiate with the Best
   Make Lots of Deals
   Close Your Deals
   Finance the Right Way
   Talk Money

Chapter 6:
Pick Pumped up People
   Pick Partners
   Human Resources: Train, Delegate, Micromanage
   Incentivize Everyone

- Build Your Team
- Don't Play Corporate Politics
- Optimize Human Resources' Communications
- Fire the Deserving
- Nature of Human Resources

Chapter 7:
Get Off Your Tuchus and Go Sell
- Contact Management
- Build a Winning Sales Team
- Win with a Rational Sales Strategy

Conclusion

PART 2 THE ENTRPRENEURSHIP PROCESS lessons

DISCLAIMER

COPYRIGHT

Copyright © 2019 All rights reserved. No part of this book may be reproduced, stored in a retrieval system, or transmitted in any form or by any means, electronic, mechanical, photocopying, recording, scanning, or otherwise, without the prior written permission of the publisher.

CHAPTER 1:
Go for the Gold

Getting started in business is the hardest part. If you had the very best start, you would have been born with a natural predisposition for business, and then your parents, teachers, and tutors would have added to your innate business sense along the way. Likewise, you would have trained at jobs, saved money to take on future competitors, and proactively taken steps to build your confidence. In this best-case scenario, you would be more adept to go out on your own since you are "ahead of the game." Besides, if your theoretical competitors had fewer financial successes, they would more than likely have less confidence and self-esteem. If you were expected to compete with these people in a profitable, burgeoning industry, you would more than likely control a greater market share and literally make millions of dollars sooner.

Nevertheless, back in reality, nothing can be perfect; nobody has perfect luck and skills, nor could they have studied and worked every day of their lives. In the business world, this truly leaves a field open for competition in almost any market space, and leaves you with years of time to study, practice and build. This can make up for any luck or genetic advantage that you may think you are missing. As long as you choose to build your self-confidence proactively, you can compete in business and in life irrespective of the past.

The most successful businesspeople are focused on a clear business plan all the time. In order to perform at this level, they tend to make sacrifices that average performers might not find acceptable. Sacrificing for your business means you may inadvertently get less sleep than your competitors, or less family and social time, or all three.

Logic suggests that without sacrifice, your business would ultimately weaken and your more aggressive competitors would continuously increase their market share at your expense. Depending on your attitude and life goals, you must decide if this type of effort is worthwhile.

Consider the plight of the average worker who reports to a superior forty hours per week while at a company where he has no personal investment and no long-term passion. This tradition of working nine-to-five for someone who will employ you for life is unlikely to be a common reality in the future and is irrelevant to a potential entrepreneur anyway.

Working for someone else is a great way to get started in the business world, but it is not where an entrepreneur with lofty goals will want to remain. Fortunately, having a high level of quality output as someone's employee will ultimately help you ascend "the corporate ladder." The more hours you spend ascending the ladder, by producing high quality work over a long duration, the more money you will be able to put away due to a combination of base salary, promotions, overtime pay and bonuses.

Your accumulation of wealth as an employee can create some padding for your family, which you can invest in a business or save to provide extra security in case of a missed paycheck. Ultimately, to maximize your take-home pay as someone else's employee, you need to work your way up to become the person who is in charge: i.e., the boss—the one who determines how the money is spent and distributed.

In addition, you can take away the knowledge, contacts and

cash that you gained as an employee to start your own business where you would get to be your own boss. In this case, your current bosses and coworkers could eventually constitute some of your new company's board of directors, board of advisors, employee pool, or shareholders.

If someone else is your boss, he will not be inclined to help you earn the absolute maximum value that your efforts can create since, by design, some of your pay directly or indirectly comes out of his and his partners' pockets. However, if you become the boss or a partner, the sky is the limit, because you will keep the maximum fair and legal amount of profit that is generated from your hard work.

Running a business in a free market, capitalist economy must be a for-profit venture or it will not be able to sustain itself and fail. A charity, on the other hand, is not for profit.

To push innovation and efficiency in your business to make as much profit as possible is moral, legal and necessary because that keeps you and your family in business and improves the economy overall, which also improves the overall health and well-being of society. Given the above, your only objective should be to maximize your financial returns diligently.

With the profits that you can make from such a straightforward business approach, you will benefit "the State" via taxes. Then, with whatever sum remain, buy the material items you desire and give generously to charity.

When you find you can free up some of your time, you can work on nonprofit endeavors, which is ultimately for the benefit of your family and our broader society. As a side effect, this is also good public relations for your business, which helps in creating a "virtuous cycle".

Keep in mind, we are not suggesting that you give away all of your time and money to charity. Instead, you should use a generous portion on the activities you feel passionate about. For example, tutoring disadvantaged children from your community, managing a charity event for a disease that afflicts your family, building a charity website, lobbying congress for disease research funding, or feeding disaster victims in Africa are all possible charitable contributions one could make. The opportunities are personal and without limitation.

To create passion for something of great significance in this world is vital for everyone, but it does not make sense for others to direct your altruistic activities. Once you are able, you get to decide how to proceed as a compassionate member of your business community. Earn plenty of money, buy whatever you feel you need for your family, and then serve your favorite causes. In effect, this creates a win-win-win situation.

BE CONFIDENT

To be a truly successful entrepreneur, there can never be any doubt in your mind that you will accomplish your goals, even if you must occasionally alter your plans to hit the same targets. Your success is as much a matter of your willpower as it is of the skills you will develop on your journey.

There are hardly any successful businesspeople, athletes, community leaders, or artists who do not feel certain of their ability to adapt and succeed. In order to achieve those results that are required to be a success, you need to fight and evolve. Your work process has to be managed as if it is a matter of survival.

Even though your attitude is focused on winning, you should not be emotionally attached to the outcome of any one transaction or activity. Cut your losses if you are certain that you've failed, because moving forward, you are going to need a clear head to achieve the highest possible volume of transactions in as instinctive a fashion as possible. This calm and confident mindset will help you focus on your exponentially expansive, efficient and evolutionary money machine.

Reliving past trials and tribulations is a drain on your mental resources. Whether the activity itself succeeded or failed, you should make a conscientious effort to learn positive lessons from everything. Don't allow the outcomes of attempted sales, deals, or employee issues harm your forward momentum or the ability to execute your plan. Your focus should be on getting the targeted outcome from each business situation rather than your emotional responses to difficulties in the process.

Your job is to make logic out of chaos: to tell people how to act quickly to solve problems but not dwell on the confusion and problems themselves. In the business world, you will find that many people won't do what they say they will do or what they should do regardless of their intentions (sometimes this includes your vendors, employees and customers). So, if you can execute successful strategies to overcome these inherent problems while maintaining balance, then you can turn chaos into a strategic advantage by playing off of your competitors' weaknesses in this area.

To achieve your highest goals, you want to be at essentially a military state of readiness and never let your guard down until the war has been won.

In virtually all industries, warriors become successful by consistently believing in themselves, toiling around the clock and testing out every promising business angle.

Winning is a self-fulfilling prophecy: if you decide to be a success, you can be.

The idea that companies have individual products that fail is really a stretch in the first place. As a whole, an unsuccessful company cannot be attributed to inanimate objects and services. Only humans have ineffective products and services, which should be considered ongoing concerns of their creators. The moment one lacks confidence in his ability to make a product evolve to a successful point is the moment it really is on a path to failure.

Certainly not every product can be saved, but failed products and services are generally the result of their creators' and managers' cognitive states. You have to make each product work by using your head to deliver what your plan calls for and by using the procedures that your company has predetermined will lead you to success.

So you need to have confidence in your plan, and that confidence will be reflected in your products, services, and ultimately, profits.

Building your confidence is an evolving process that starts by saying to yourself, "I believe I can win."

If you haven't tried a logical business concept to the best of your ability, don't assume the idea itself won't work. In fact, most concepts are sound in theory but not executed according to their original plans. When this happens, no excuses will suffice, nor will they help to solve the problem or reverse the failure. The only option that will work is rational and decisive action.

Starting modestly while steadily evolving your business concepts can ultimately help you understand how to accomplish your goals. A key to your small tests is to get the processes rolling quickly and get through all the embarrassing mistakes so you can improve rapidly. It is important to realize that failure and rejection are required for success. You have to dare to fail every day. Keeping too safe isn't really a safe long-term strategy. Granted, it will spare you some loss and embarrassment (i.e., from going one-step back) but at the expense of the compounding growth you require (two steps forward). Tempered risk along with good decision-making is the path to high rewards.

Many unsuccessful business ideas could have worked, if they had been properly optimized and leveraged. For example, Google and Yahoo are still thriving while AltaVista fell by the wayside. At one point, they were on par; however, AltaVista apparently didn't have enough confidence or the ability to execute their own business model. In hindsight, we believe if they had moved forward more confidently, like their now billionaire peers, Alta Vista possibly could have been as successful as Google.

There are few secrets in business; nothing is being hidden from you. The methods of developing better business practices are clear if you are looking for them.

BE A MACHINE

Those who work harder will be more profitable overall. We are not claiming that working "harder" is more advantageous than working "smarter." You actually need to work harder with more raw man-hours AND work smarter by using evolving Best Practices to maximize your financial gain. Unlike the majority of business strategies, which are mostly theoretical, this is a mathematically sound principle that works virtually every time. The good news is that it applies to everyone and can seemingly work miracles. So if you are trying to evolve your business faster than your competition, one way to produce more, be more efficient and get a critical jump on those competitors is by putting in longer, harder hours of labor.

For example, a person who works eighty hours a week instead of forty is not necessarily twice as profitable proportionally; she's more than likely three times as profitable due to economies of scale gained from focused work time. In the charitable world, someone who works twice as many hours could help three times as many people compared to their "competitor." A naturally better worker could be even more than three times effective.

Even though working heavy hours is essential on the path to success, some may feel this particular aspect of business is not worth the sacrifice. Undertaking the responsibility of business management is a personal decision. In this case, and throughout this book, we are simply disclosing methods of those who have been successful. Whether or not it's a good idea to attempt to follow in their footsteps is up to you.

Aside from a good work ethic, a realistic general plan or a comprehensive written business plan will ultimately facilitate positive results—provided you actually follow it closely. Much of society is already working hard, but if they were to work more hours and apply themselves to a serious plan, they could achieve the lives of their dreams.

Fledgling businesspeople often don't realize how close they are to a major success. In most cases, success is just around the corner with a few years of hard work applied properly to their industry. Many people may not recognize the weaknesses or complacencies in their competition. They could easily underestimate the size of their global market, or they might not understand that with a couple of extra hours of work per day, they could uncover and develop ideas that would produce large new advances in corporate productivity.

Competitors often work just hard enough to stay on par or barely above the rest. So if your team makes an aggressive push forward in the marketplace, the competition could easily be blindsided and fall behind. Your top business competitors might feel they don't need to try their hardest because too many other possible competitors, like you, don't step up to the plate.

The more hours that you work early on, the more money you will be able to put away in order to invest in a new business or provide cash flow for your family. In a new business, you might not be paid for a while, so the padding created from long hours at your last "job" is critical.

Once you are ahead there should be no turning back. Remain at full speed until you exit your market by either selling your company, merging with another company, going public, or letting your underlings take control—or just live on the dividends (distributions of profits) and pass them on to your children. The compounding effects of your efforts will bring you more money faster, thereby creating more leverage and freedom to use how and when you choose for your next charity or business project.

If invested carefully, the extra money you put away year after year from all your overtime labor will compound. Compounding produces a snowball effect because interest earnings grow from an ever-increasing baseline each year as long as you reinvest the distributions and dividends. The effect of compounding is that extra earnings continue to rise each successive year unlike simple interest monies that don't compound.

Overall, hard work might not be the only disparity separating the rich from the poor, but it certainly enhances any other advantages the average professional brings to the economic table. Lawyers, doctors and other high-end professionals, for example, make more money than most partly because they've put in more hours in school and at work.

Working hard isn't easy by definition, yet understanding the processes that lead to success is right at your fingertips. Pay attention to the ideas that are being offered informally all around you: by mentors, in books and periodicals, on business TV and radio, and especially all over the Internet. However, make sure you filter for just the best information out of the masses. By putting in the time to do proper research you will find most of what you need is freely accessible.

Spending peaceful time contemplating all of your options to see how they fit together and then "gaming" out every possible success scenario will help you make better decisions. Creating flowcharts can be helpful because, in theory, it allows you to understand all your options and their possible respective results, helping you choose your best bets to pursue.

In running your business, doing the actual work involved may entail long hours and some stress. On the other hand, this could also empower you to retire in a third of the amount of time it would normally take—and that could allow for a more relaxing second half of your life. Here's how: if you are working twice as many hours and gaining the added efficiency that scale offers, you are likely to be three times as productive. Therefore, you should make three times more money in that same period and potentially retire in a third of the time. One successful businessman was quoted as saying, "You get to work half days the rest of your life. Any 12 hours will do." We think instead you can possibly work half days for just 1/3 of your life.

Being successful in business is not necessarily an easier life for you. In the long run, however, it could be more rewarding and fun. So get to it! Don't procrastinate on the difficult projects ahead; hopefully, your competitors are doing just that. You will be better prepared for the future if you proactively take hold of the present.

BE CHARITABLE

We believe a charity should operate like a for-profit business. The main difference should be that the focus of the organization and the metrics (key data), which are being managed, should highlight the number of "needy" stakeholders being well served rather than the numbers of dollars of profits.

In business, one only has to count cash to know how well they are doing, which is fairly easy. To help people other than yourself in a meaningful way is much harder to address and quantify, but it should be approached with equal vigor.

Charities do not distribute profits or have stock shares. All of what ordinarily would be profit from their business-like activities should be redirected back into their nonprofit projects. In a properly run 501c3 charity, there are generally staff members who receive modest salaries and other ordinary business expenses, but high salaries and expenses are frowned upon, and even illegal in some cases.

Other sorts of charities, such as churches, associations and political organizations, fall into different tax classes, whereas here, we are focused on fully tax-exempt 501c3 organizations, which are essentially charitable businesses whose monies flow internally after being raised or earned. There are no shareholders, dividends, or stock sales in a 501c3.

No one should directly profit from charitable activities, yet there are abhorrent cases where there have been executive excess at the expense of charity stakeholders and society. One high profile example is the recent discovery that an executive at United Way was misappropriating funds. This is an anomaly and not in the spirit of charity. Cases like this should be prosecuted to the full extent of the law. Furthermore, to use charitable donations on anything other than direct charitable actions and modest expenses (to run and grow an organization) is a moral violation.

Some corporate vendors who serve charities naturally profit since they aren't nonprofit organizations, but their profits should be limited by managers on both sides of the transaction.

Although this is a business book, we truly believe that a life with family and charity as the core is better than a life focused on business. Our goal is to teach you how to get the best out of both. We want you and as many other people, companies, and organizations as possible to produce as much as possible, so more spare money and time is created to help other people and causes when you aren't spending quality time with family and friends.

If you need even more convincing as to why you should optimize your work product, consider how extra income can help you send your kids to better colleges, or allow you to take an extra week per year of vacation, or renovate part of your home, or even allow you to buy a new iPhone—if that's your thing.

Once you get past the thrill of attaining material possessions, give away as much as you can safely afford to your favorite nonprofits or put it in a charitable trust, donor advised fund or foundation for later.

For a person who successfully follows our business advice and scores big, we recommend committing 15-30% of your wealth to nonprofit interests and about 50% of your available time. Since we are only recommending you do this after you are wealthy, it couldn't hurt you and will definitely give your life extra meaning.

If you create extra financial padding, you can essentially buy your time back, and if you desire, donate some spare time and

Dr. Dennis Mulumba

cash to whichever charities you choose.

BE A SUCCESS

In 1999, Stanford graduate Charles Brewer, founder of the Internet provider MindSpring, attributed his success to "honesty, integrity, frugality and adherence to the Golden Rule [to be friendly, courteous, fair and compassionate – Do unto others as you'd have them do unto you]."

Creating and maintaining core values as Brewer has is essential to having the most cohesive organization and trustworthy brand. Moreover, expressing your values openly with your employees creates a sense of security, and this in turn will truly make your company more secure.

Avoid blaming external forces or people for problems that are in your own best interest to solve, irrespective of how they emerged. Blaming the economy will never help you, nor will blaming the government, a political party, your mom, your teachers, your competitors, your genetic code, your community, or your boss.

Even if it is ostensibly true, claiming you have had bad luck or that others are at fault for your issues will never help you achieve a winning attitude for the future.

The world offers an enormous and ever-expanding global economy; all you need is a minuscule piece of that economy to succeed or a slightly larger slice of your local economy.

Nobody and nothing can stop you from getting your fair market share if you maintain a long term focused effort. Therefore, if you happen to be out of work or aren't earning enough and you think there is an external force to blame, then at the very least, you should be proactively working to change that force every day, as opposed to complaining about it.

Very few people who start a business from scratch and succeed can attribute their success to luck. Of course, a small portion of society is born into a family business or is undeservedly promoted in a big company, which is a small barrier for competitors. Overall, successful people are those who are focused on proactively performing clear goals, at the highest level, for the most hours, over the longest duration.

The good news is if you want to be wealthy, you should take to heart that all the other rich people who surround you have 99.9% the same DNA as you. The difference is not in their genes or in their luck: they just chose to succeed in business and proceed accordingly.

Don't get lost with intangible plans and tasks. Instead, stay focused on tangible long-term goals, while understanding what's truly happening around you minute-by-minute, and how you can positively affect it.

BE THERE AND BE AWARE

Simply by being "in the game" and being serious about trying to succeed will help you win 50% of your competitive battles, and therefore account for half of your success. This is because most theoretically able-bodied workers are apprehensive to fight, and therefore are not well-suited to win while conducting "competitive" commerce on a daily basis.

Working long, hard hours every day, accounts for about another 40% of one's success, and choosing the right industry is probably responsible for another 8%. In our estimation, luck only accounts for about 2% of the success of proactive entrepreneurs.

So get over the notion of good luck being a reason why people might win in a business environment. Even if luck is an element, it is an uncontrollable one and a minor one. Focus instead on the majority of factors, which can truly be improved daily by your best efforts.

More specifically, if your business is run by hard workers like you who show up every day ready for their tasks and pay close attention to business details and emerging opportunities, you will have a much higher chance of long-term success than could be attributable to luck.

Keep in mind that the smartest people are not always on top. In reality, the person who believes in himself or herself the most, irrespective of their nominal brainpower, is usually the most successful.

You have probably heard the expression, "He's smart, but he doesn't apply himself." This is not a beneficial way to go through school. In business, however, if you feel you aren't the smartest, then you should make up for it by changing the rules, which you couldn't have done at school. This would be akin to getting yourself a new teacher, selecting your own schoolbooks, choosing new classmates (teammates), changing school hours, getting leveraged (student) financing, merging and deleting classes at will, or beating up on your peers who were born with higher IQs but are complacent.

You can see that each idea would have helped you be the leader in your class (even if a bit heavy-handed) and is analogous to how you can still lead in the business world. If you could have changed the rules like this in class, you could have attained straight A's. Fortunately, in business, you are allowed to change all the rules to get top grades as long as you don't run astray of any laws.

You don't have to be the smartest to dominate your business niche, but you do have to be among the most assertive and confident.

Attention to detail is one of the most essential qualities that you can develop while you become a leader. Anything that isn't done completely and correctly will have to be reworked, thereby wasting time and money. If you are not detailed, you are likely to initiate cascading problems that could put you out of business before you have a chance to recover.

Indeed, bad detail in accounting could land you in tax court. Bad detail in law could land your client in jail, and if you are a doctor, you could accidentally kill someone. Bad detail when reviewing references could leave you with an employee who embarrasses you and drains your profits. Bad detail with security could get your store robbed or could facilitate the theft of credit card numbers from your e-commerce web site.

In short, if business areas are not studied and managed in detail, harmful patterns can perpetuate.

Having a sincere respect for time is crucial, too. Since the chance for short-term success in any business is slim, working with a limited time horizon would be corporate suicide.

Equally wrongheaded would be trying to target your "exit strategy" to a short calendar window. Companies should run or appear to run as if they intend to be in business for a hundred years, not as if the management is ready to run out the door by selling or folding the company or getting better jobs (regardless if that is really the case).

Most people are generally focused on their next paycheck, not necessarily on what they could accomplish over longer periods. This is understandable but is still a detrimental mindset to a potentially independent businessperson.

Instead, you should be looking forward over a long time frame, even though you are working day-to-day and minute-to-minute on your high priority tasks. Moreover, you should be thinking about what will happen if you reinforce a sound business strategy consistently over time. Usually, a long-term and focused effort will pay off; short-term get-rich-quick schemes will not. Respect the fact that business leaders usually put in years of dedicated labor to reach their high positions—and you can, too, if you choose.

Finally, it is essential to know how to multitask. Time is everything, and every second counts. As a result, you will have no choice but to attempt to overlap your tasks. This can be tricky since you may not have enough attention at the right place at the right time.

The need to focus contradicts the need to overlap, however, you can strive to create an optimized balance. Multitasking might be as simple as wearing a headset when you are on the phone, so if you are on hold, you can do other work. Other forms of multitasking could include talking on speakerphone while you drive (carefully!), or working while you are in the airport or on a plane, or typing notes on a contact manager while you talk. Even worse, you could read draft contracts while your family sleeps on vacation, if you're up to it.

The reason for multitasking is to optimize your time by accomplishing two or more goals simultaneously rather than accomplishing one task at the expense of others. Multitask where it can be effective and won't harm your other initiatives. This is a great way to assist your competitors in falling behind.

BE THE EDGE

The best ideas and the most sensible ideas are the ones that are not contrived. This is why people always say, "Why didn't I think of that?"

In order to achieve a winning edge—the element that separates you from the rest of the pack and ensures your success in business—you will have to find ways to identify good ideas and develop them quickly and effectively.

Once you've selected or invented a business idea, you should review it from many different angles. With this insight, you can create numerous small business tests in search of the most profitable. We suggest trying higher risk ideas with potentially high rewards along with those that are generally lower-risk, tried and true moneymakers.

This process will help identify future profit centers that are worth pursuing. If you are simultaneously trying out many angles and reinforcing ones that work best in an upward spiral, then you will be creating downside protection.

If your competitor is more adept than you are, she might be able to wipe out one of your profit centers. However, if you have spent many years growing and reinforcing several profit centers, then losing in one area will not make your competitor superior nor will it ultimately harm your business.

Intuitively, you should know that competitors in a free market, capitalist economy are going to try to "take you out." You must improve and prepare every day for the inevitable commercial "war."

So long as you've been working harder and smarter and aligning yourself with good partners, employees and suppliers, you can survive at the expense of, or in cooperation with, all those who compete.

Competitors and insider stakeholders who doubt you and your abilities are predictable obstacles that every businessperson has to navigate. Other jealous, doubtful, or unmotivated people who are close to you personally or on the competitor's side will constantly try to get in your way, break you down, or challenge you. Regardless, your job is to produce in your marketplace while all your challengers remain personally distracted by you and your success.

You will find an uncomfortably large portion of the workforce and society overall has a sense of entitlement, wants something for nothing, has no sense of urgency, works only on their own agendas, has inflated self-worth, is not appropriately competitive, and lacks truthful analysis and reflection of their past actions and business plans. These sorts of people are most likely to disturb your trail to the top.

In addition, since a lot of trouble tends to come from the inside, in today's business climate, it may be wiser to hire people as subcontractors for some time before considering them as employees.

Like athletes in the Olympics, the people who train the hardest on one goal and prove to be the most adept will win, or at least get to share the top prizes. Others who can't manage to get past the competition will be run off and knocked down. By maintaining your focus, distractions and detractors will harm your competitor's business more than your own.

Paradoxically, everything that is difficult in business is ultimately for the good because it is yet another obstacle for your competitor that you intend to overcome more effectively. In the quest to grow your businesses, you will constantly discover new, difficult, and unpredictable challenges. Whether you find those challenges to be blessings or curses is just a matter of perspective. Without obstacles, there would be no barriers to entry for competitors, and your market could become saturated and unprofitable quickly. Obstacles allow you to practice and learn from each task in context, and help you learn how to hurdle obstacles in general, which is leverage that you can use for the future.

The more obstacles there are in your industry, the more areas there are for you to master better and faster than the competition. This will place you even further in front of the pack. Were there fewer industry obstacles, competitors would have a better chance at stealing market share at your expense. Therefore, the challenges, barriers, and difficulties in business are beneficial to confident, proactive entrepreneurs like you.

CHAPTER 2:
Make a Winning Plan

When choosing the type of company you want to operate, selecting from an area where you have previously worked or studied can be extremely advantageous. This can save you considerable time and will obviously hold more of your interest. Yet, if such an area does not offer the highest long-term financial gain, it may be best to choose another path early on.

From a business perspective, training to work in a field that you are passionate about would be your initial "Best Bet" as opposed to investing your time in something where you have no personal affinity.

Peter Lynch of Fidelity Magellan Fund put forth the mantra, "Invest in what you know or what is near to you." Ostensibly, to invest in something you do not understand would be folly. Warren Buffet invests in the same way, as you can tell from his investments in See's Candies, Coca-Cola, and Dairy Queen, and even his local Omaha jewelry distributor, Borsheim's.

Spending your life training for one particular type of business would probably not be easy or always fun and this may not be the right path for you. Nevertheless, if you were to do so, there is usually a significant financial benefit. Then again, if you did train for much of your life in one area, there is no assurance you wouldn't eventually decide to abandon that field and concept for any number of valid reasons. Fortunately, there are additional great career options.

So if you haven't trained your life for one business (i.e., your Best Bet), your Second Best Bet would be to go into a line of business that you are personally attracted to even if you are not currently experienced in that area. For example, if you have a natural affinity for motorcycles, and identified an under-served market, then starting a motorcycle dealership could be a good choice for you. Choosing an area of personal interest is likely to be a fulfilling option. As a result, you may learn more, work harder, and stay with the industry longer, thereby making more money faster than you would in a boring job.

Finally, a Third Bet, which fits most new business candidates (if you are not applying your First or Second Best Bet), would be to choose a relatively random line of business after exhaustively studying research and financial models on emerging industries, even if you have no personal interest or history in that particular line of business.

Be creative. Pick an industry that is not fully developed but has a lot of potential. Think about less sophisticated or glamorous business niches since they are more likely to be overlooked by potential competitors.

Another option would be to consider niches of big industries. For example, instead of trying to be the leader of the "widget" industry, strive to be the leading analyst of the industry or the leading supplier of specialty marketing services. You should be spending huge amounts of time considering every creative element that might suit your future interests, and then you can bet on the most realistic of those options. Fantasize about your future, and then come down to earth and carry on with business.

We also recommend that you read profusely so you can better understand your opportunities: namely broad business periodicals, your own trade journals, and local business press. Some national names to consider are The Economist, Fortune, Forbes, Wall Street Journal, Business Week, Washington Post and The New York Times; the local business sections of other newspapers, and even fluff magazines like Entrepreneur and Inc, which still hint at hot opportunities despite some shallow self-serving "reporting".

Financial television and radio shows like Bloomberg, CNBC, and Fox Business also uncover many emerging business concepts, and their proponents, that are often worthy of review. They regularly interview the world's richest and smartest businesspeople who have a lot of value to share. Record the shows, watch them intently, and learn from them.

Nowadays FaceBook, Twitter, blogs, newsgroups, email lists, social networks, and other Web 2.0 communications media are the most up-to-date areas to learn about business and share information.

Most importantly, you should study the industry publications that are dealing with the specific business areas you are considering. Over a long period, you should keep your eyes and ears open for all types of ideas. This informal research will lead to areas worthy of intensive research.

It is also important to create and execute market surveys prior to entering any particular business area. Find as many of your potential marketing targets as possible and give them an incentive to complete a well-thought out survey. When you analyze the results, you should have valuable information to guide your decisions. The larger the pool of people surveyed, the greater insight you are likely to gain about your future market. You can easily outsource this function.

If you do ample research and discuss your plans with a variety of lay and professional people, you will be guided towards your best courses of action. If you conduct surveys in the manner described, your risk will diminish, and a preponderance of your financial bets will be based on educated decision-making rather than random risk.

Among other powerful ideas, Peters stresses that your entire proactive business team adds little bits of value into your business continuously and doesn't ever rest on its laurels.

Besides tried and true business authors, we recommend you review the media and participate with emerging business minds, whose writings can often be found online in blogs or linked to various forums and sites like Facebook, Twitter, YouTube, Technorati and LinkedIn.

To further your progress you could take speed-reading courses, which may help triple the speed you consume valuable information.

PLAN YOUR SUCCESS IN WRITING

Consider many possible scenarios for each business before you actually choose the one that you want to start. Once you decide what corporate niche to assault, the next step is to create a written business plan. This should be relatively simple and as short as possible, without overlooking any key components. Pro-forma financial statements estimating the company's future success should be based on realistic assumptions that are explained in notations and attached to your plan. Take courses in Accounting 101, Excel, and PowerPoint to get started.

In the initial drafting of your business plan, it is beneficial to identify your audience for the plan and craft your message accordingly; decide if the documentation is intended to be studied just by you, by your staff and management, by potential outside investors, or by the public at large in some cases.

If you are premature with your big idea and just need some talking points for background consultants, rather than writing a full-blown "business plan," you could instead write a "business model" in a few short pages. If necessary, you can create multiple versions of your documentation to meet the interests of various classes of potential stakeholders.

There are standard boilerplate forms for business plans available online, which are acceptable for simple plans and small investors; however, larger investors will prefer a thorough and clearly worded original document with detailed justifications for your assumptions, something that summarizes specific research that you have done in your industry.

Investors may want to review and approve the proposed staff, the marketplace, the math, and other select planning items mentioned in your plans before they agree to invest. This is why a complete business plan is best when approaching potential investors.

Among other things, your business plan should document the expected startup costs and the costs to operate the business until it hits a "break-even" point. This will help reveal the level of financing that you require.

It is essential to truly believe in your mission. Merely acting as though you are a believer is not enough. Don't start a business unless you can put in the required effort happily and willingly to make your dream a reality. If you lack enthusiasm and confidence, then you cannot display those attributes to your potential investors, staff, customers, or the community at large. Your competitors will intuitively sense your apathy and take advantage of any weaknesses you reveal before you get the opportunity to control your fair share of the market.

However, if you have a well-written business plan, adequate financing, boundless energy, and a willingness to make fast changes in a fluid environment, then congratulations, you have what it takes to be a business leader!

QUIT YOUR JOB

After you have determined what type of business you want to pursue, written a business plan, and secured some basic financing, you will then need to take the next big step and quit your current job.

There is practically no way to build a seriously profitable business on a part-time basis. As we stated in Chapter 1, raw man-hours often prove to be a key to success, and in order to make a proper go of it, you must be as focused as possible on your singular business goal.

It is critical that you attempt to keep good relations with your former bosses and co-workers. Odds are you will run across them again as customers, suppliers, new co-workers, neighbors, references, or industry competitors. Regardless, you will inevitably work with other people who know them. The last thing you need is the strategic disadvantage of people souring your reputation behind your back. So you should always end relationships on positive terms and keep in touch with all contacts that may benefit you or your new company in the future.

There will always be some people in your life who will try to discourage you from quitting your secure position when you want to start out on your own. The truth of the matter is that doing this is a big risk. But what is the worst thing that could happen? If you're smart, you won't let yourself get to the point of homelessness and destitution before you realize your plan has not worked, and then you could put yourself back on the job market. In the worst-case scenario, you still will have learned many valuable lessons that can be properly applied to your future.

We believe that if you have solid motivational drive, irrespective of your past, you could start at even an entry-level position and still make it to the top of your industry, given enough time. Make sure your boss's plans for you are the same as your own, and make sure that you assertively earn, and explicitly ask for, your promotions along the way.

If you can't be promoted at your current gig, you can keep looking for better employment until you find the most suitable match with someone who will give you the opportunities you deserve and are willing to earn. If you are well-studied and proactive, someone will recognize your work ethic and the results you could potentially achieve for their team. From there, you could be hired and on your way up the corporate ladder.

You could possibly keep moving up the ladder until your boss becomes your business partner or until you venture out on your own with your new skills, using your sweat equity and network of contacts to build a larger, more sustainable income.

The point is that you are never out of the game irrespective of any hardships. You can stay motivated and keep picking up the pieces, wherever they may have fallen in the past. Persistence and practice will move you in a positive direction. Being knocked back often may not be desirable, but it does not ruin your long-term prospects either.

Consider the stock market. Despite many market crashes in the last century, most long-term investors have profited handsomely. Likewise, if you are a committed entrepreneur and follow rational business practices day after day, you, too, will eventually succeed—even if the business environment occasionally appears to work against you or has radical fluctuations over time. There is no doubt that you will often feel like you are taking a step back, but given our mutual three steps forward approach, you will still end up considerably ahead.

Dr. Dennis Mulumba

You can't be scared to be a capitalist in a capitalist society. It's not wrong to profit or make money from your business peers and your community. Ultimately, within the flows of the economy, they, too, make it from you, your family, and your peers. Everyone deserves to make an honest buck. Profits create a virtuous cycle if you work with virtuous individuals during the process in a free and fair market economy.

This is the way American society and its market economy is fueled. No capitalism would mean no jobs, no nice cars, no rent money, etc. Capitalism is a key to a healthy democratic society. Moreover, in our case and throughout this book, we believe the end goal in creating wealth is ultimately to channel it towards social actions. Thus, there is no reason to avoid or fear capitalism. Just dig in!

GET INCORPORATED AND SITUATED

So by now, you are on your way with a business plan in hand and newfound free time to start your company. The next step is to hire a lawyer and other professionals because in order to operate properly there is a tremendous volume of documents to be processed and submitted in a timely fashion. This unavoidable bureaucracy could easily paralyze any business if not done properly.

It is critical to have a great lawyer who will expedite your paperwork and bail you out of some of the complexities in business. At first, you may find that hiring outside counsel hourly is too expensive for your small business. In this case, you should try to have a multi-disciplined lawyer, preferably a generalist with a business edge, directly on your team. This person can perform many management and legal functions and can serve as "General Counsel" if he is qualified.

We have found that over a long period, an early employees' option to accept stock, stock options, and other good quality incentives in a successful company will become worth much more than their hourly wages. If your company is not already successful, or has not already raised considerable funds, then most likely it cannot afford professional salaries anyway. Low salaries and heavy incentives for hard workers is one of the best broad strategies you can adopt in making your company successful. With this in mind, the lawyer on your team could get paid predominantly with incentive pay like stock options, and therein agree to accept lower nominal wages, which would help finance the company by not draining the bank account in the early years. You could apply this same incentive-heavy recruitment strategy when hiring an accountant, computer engineer, or other professionals that you may require.

Furthermore, you can attempt to help defray other ordinary cash expenses for any vendor or partner by offering any of a wide variety of incentives that directly correlate with your own business success. Having an aggressive lawyer and other professionals aligned with your financial best interests cannot hurt you, unless you overpay. You should interview a number of professional vendors and choose the ones you favor. From that short list, determine if any of them are interested in your alternate payment arrangement. Certainly, the more past successes you've had, the more likely they are to bite.

THE NAMING PROCESS

Next will be the critical step of picking the right name for your business. The significance of this decision cannot be underestimated.

Among the best remembered names are double entendres (phrases with double meanings) which are often whimsical. One meaning is pertinent to your industry or company, and the other meaning is often silly or otherwise memorable.

It is also favorable if your name makes use of alliteration like "TotallyTwisted" for a pretzel company, or "WebWave" for a marine-related web site. A rhyming name could also be positive like DupreesTrees or MellowYellow. You might also consider having your company name begin with the letter "A" to get to the top of alphabetical listings or "Z" to be particularly memorable. You can also mix and match these attributes in an attempt to create an optimized balance.

Nevertheless, you may not find a name that you and your stakeholders like with these characteristics included, but to ensure you ultimately make the best decision, spend a lot of time studying your options. Also, get votes and opinions on your top name options from as many people as possible including from crowdsources. If you find consensus in a name, then it is likely to be a great choice. In this case you could add naming questions and voting as part of your market survey process mentioned earlier in this book. At the end of the day, make sure you and your direct stakeholders feel comfortable with your final naming decision whatever it may be.

Before you go forward with the name, be sure that you can buy the ".com" Internet domain name that is an exact match. For instance, don't name your company TotallyTwisted if you cannot buy totallytwisted.com to use for branding reinforcement. Doing so would be a failure from which you would never fully recover. Getting totallytwisted. net will not suffice because your brand would always be at risk of dilution by the primary Internet brand holder, which is always whoever owns the exact ".com" extension for any word, phrase, or company name.

In addition, the name of your business (and therefore your domain and all of your branding) should be consistent, easy to say, easy to spell, and easy to remember.

You should also be able to trademark (TM) it via the US Patent and Trademark Office if it is not a generic descriptive industry term. Be sure someone else hasn't placed your name in line at the USPTO before you invest in your own business with that same branded name. If you believe that you have the first rights to that expression, you could invest in counsel to fight the other parties, utilizing the trademark process to gain legal control of that expression in your market space. You can locate information on filing trademarks and review existing marks and applications from the US Patent and Trademark Office at www.uspto.gov, but you will probably require legal counsel nonetheless.

A couple of things to keep in mind:

(a) To get a trademark, the name cannot actually describe the product. For example, you cannot call your company Hot Pancakes if you are actually selling pancakes because that would preclude other pancake companies from using that same basic terminology in marketing which would be unfair. Conversely, if you named your brand of auto parts Hot Pancakes, you would likely qualify to get the trademark. Then others in the auto parts industry could not use the words Hot Pancakes in their marketing since you gained legal control of that non-descriptive terminology first. You can protect non-descriptive terms like Hot Pancakes for auto parts, but you can't protect descriptive terms like Hot Pancakes for a pancake company.

(b) There can be no other trademarks similar to yours that are already successfully registered or in line to be registered. So don't name your company TotallyTwisted if you can't register that identical trademark for your service. Again, you need the ".com" domain also (in this case totallytwisted.com) to go with your company name.

LOGOS AND SLOGANS

For marketing purposes, you usually want to choose an appropriate slogan to go with your name, like "Twist and Shout" for a pretzel company, or "Ride the Wave" for a marine company, or "Just Do It" for a sports shoe company.

You also need a logo: a graphical representation of your brand like the famous Nike "swoosh" symbol or the default Coca-Cola lettering. FYI: a logo and slogan is "trademarkable" if it is unique but it is not "patentable" or "copyrightable". In the case of Coca-Cola, their formula would be patentable and their literal wording would be copyrightable. Conversely, it is logos, slogans, lettering, and colors that get trademarks.

In the vetting process for your brand, each element of your logo, slogan, font and so on should be carefully considered with the help of marketing professionals, and then ultimately selected from as many options as you can afford from professional graphic designers.

You need to have a first class logo, and then ensure your logo has perpetual and extensive exposure in your target market, which in some cases are all the world's Internet consumers.

Your marketing material preceded with your name, slogan, and logo (which may or may not include a graphical symbol to go with your style of text treatment) should be exposed in a wide variety of venues simultaneously: referrals, press articles, sales messages, affinity groups, and materials via fax, mail, newspaper ads, radio, on-line, and so forth. We like to use the expression "tag the world."

Your brand is everything so don't shortchange it. In the beginning, pay to build it by leveraging the right image and domain, and stick with it, because you will discover that branding reinforcement over a long term also pays out for the long term.

Now you are ready for your lawyer to compile and then file basic paperwork to get your business properly incorporated and legally operational in the marketplace.

Basic filings and documents you will require include:

- ✓ A federal ID number from the IRS
- ✓ Articles of Incorporation
- ✓ A "fictitious name" filing (the name you would like to register in your state)
- ✓ Shareholder Operating Agreements
- ✓ Stock Subscription Agreements
- ✓ Stock Option Agreements
- ✓ Stock Certificates
- ✓ A Corporate Seal

In fact, you should plan to have this additional material also:

For Marketing:

- ✓ Name and slogan options
- ✓ Domain names (your primary brand plus singulars, plurals, misspellings, ".net" version, subsidiary names, etc.)
- ✓ Logo options
- ✓ Web content
- ✓ Business card templates
- ✓ Contact management system and backups
- ✓ Sales texts that can be copied and pasted between media
- ✓ Proposal templates
- ✓ Print flyers
- ✓ Fax cover template/letterhead template
- ✓ E-mail text templates and signature text

For Management:

- ✓ Business model for internal purposes

- ✓ Staff contact directory
- ✓ Standard Operating Procedures (SOPs)
- ✓ Mission statement
- ✓ Backed up file systems including contact manager and PC configurations
- ✓ For Investors:
- ✓ Private Placement Memoranda (PPM)
- ✓ Business plan or model
- ✓ Business presentations in PowerPoint and Flash
- ✓ Merger agreements
- ✓ Asset purchase agreements

For Legal:

- ✓ Nondisclosure and non-compete agreements
- ✓ Proprietary inventions agreements
- ✓ Legal agreement templates
- ✓ Domain details and other intellectual property

For Financial:

- ✓ QuickBooks backups
- ✓ Monthly financial statements

MAKE PROGRESS

Without actually seeing any numbers, you can often tell which companies are successful, or will become so in the near future. One way is by looking into the offices of a small and young business, which can be very revealing. If there is a lot of activity going on, it's a good sign. It may take a while to make hard profits, but if the phone is ringing and you have important meetings regularly, then you are probably on the right path. Any office where there is energy, where people are being hired, and many meetings are taking place, is an office moving in the right direction.

If you ever think your business is standing idle, you are wrong. For a business, standing still really indicates that it is going backward relative to the well-heeled competition.

When there is energy and activity, it shows the entrepreneurs are doing everything they can to make sure their products and services are getting as much exposure as possible, and in the greatest variety of ways possible.

To illustrate the exponential value and power created by making proactive business improvements, consider if you were to enhance just one small aspect of your operation every day, in 5 years you would have over 1500 improvements. Presumably, some of those tweaks to your business will be significantly profitable if you have stayed focused on the items that appear to offer the highest yield based on your studies and discussions, or the "lowest hanging fruit," which could become readily convertible to cash.

Conversely, if one of your competitors who wants a more relaxed lifestyle decides to improve one item merely every third day, at the end of 5 years, he will have just over 500 tweaks.

So with more than 1000 additional improvements to your business than your competitor, you will have a much more profitable operation due to the many added efficiencies and opportunities. Remember, there is always a means to improve and expand an already good product and its marketing. Overall, everything in your company will be a work in progress, which means you always have additional opportunity to grow successfully.

In business and society, saving money is a natural obsession. Yet in order to be successful in your business, you are going to have to spend money to make money. Companies can spend far too much energy on cutting costs. Instead, you should focus on assertively enhancing your sales and marketing systems, since managing expenses should be intrinsic to every businessperson, and overdoing it offers scant value. Heads of companies often spend more time and money than necessary when contemplating and negotiating ways to cut costs, and they are therefore losing lots of opportunities in the process.

When you pull yourself and your employees away from the daily tasks to discuss saving money, and there is really none to save, you are instead wasting money and wasting your and your employees' time. This is counterproductive to achieving your goals of financial success and is too stressful on your company. You ultimately will have to let go of money and control to invest further into your business as opposed to just saving money. Management activities should mostly be based on longer-term and broader goals, even if they are at the expense of short-term financial opportunities. Another way to look at this is that if you are always saving money instead of making money, then you won't have any left to save.

Your energies are better spent on taking the costly activities that occur in your business, improving them to become ever more valuable, and applying the new processes learned to your Best Practices manual. When you focus on enhancing each day-to-day operational method that takes place in your business, including consistently addressing the quality of your products and services, your cost structures, and your customer service, you will ultimately make your company exceptionally profitable, efficient, and reliable.

CHAPTER 3:
Best Practices as Weapons

From Day One, it is important to document what works best for you and your company, i.e., your Best Practices and Standard Operating Procedures (SOPs). This book is our medium for documenting our own Best Practices; we encourage you to adopt as many as you see fit while sharing them and adding whatever else you develop or discover independently.

There is no set limit to your Best Practices arsenal; it is a continually evolving and fluid document. Old ideas should be thrown out now and again while new ones are readily added. Some ideas can simply be added to your normal business flow, yet there may be times when you are so overworked that some emerging and innovative ideas cannot be as easily implemented and have to be saved for later.

After preparing extensive documentation about the Best Practices that drive your industry and your company, you should then create Standard Operating Procedures that explain how to do all the theoretical tasks in an organized manner.

Equally important is to keep a fluid To-Do list of up to a hundred tasks of varying sizes that you should manage with approximate completion dates. Your list should constantly be reprioritized and many of the tasks should be delegated as part of your plan to scale your organization. Meanwhile, higher-level tasks can be added for you and the executive team, so the cycle will be repeated, therefore creating an ever-expanding upward spiral.

Your contact management system can help organize some of these activities in a simple manner through the built-in calendar and its many goal-oriented functions. This is key.

All tasks, however difficult they may be, must be well-documented and prioritized for future implementation. It is okay to put something on hold, but do not leave it off your To-Do list or skip it altogether. If the task has made your list, then you have prequalified it as a viable idea, so why ignore a viable, potentially profitable advancement in your company. It is merely a notation on your To-Do list that you can study and implement later or delete if it appears impractical after further study.

Documenting the procedures that you use for each part of your business is extremely important. While you strive for constant incremental improvements in your processes, update the documentation accordingly. Following this method creates an easy path to train people under you, so you can delegate tasks that are ever more profitable while focusing more of your own time on creating new opportunities.

You are starting at the top of the ladder while each person to whom you have delegated tasks is working his way up from the bottom. The object is to delegate as much as possible in order for your staff to rise closer toward the top. Then they can hire new workers to replace themselves. This allows you to consistently raise the bar and focus on only the most profitable and highest priority deal-closing activities, which is one of your keys to wealth.

The Best Practices information and the Standard Operating Procedures manuals that you develop then need to be combined into a Training Manual for all new employees and used as a continuing education opportunity for existing employees. Creating the manual could be as simple as copying and pasting the best information that you have already compiled over time or as complex as detailed "Flash" and "PowerPoint" presentations and competency tests.

Many of the creative processes that are required in the business world can't be reduced to steps in your Standard Operating Procedures manual; however, it is still necessary to attempt to document what works and continuously add to this set of information. The Best Practices and Standard Operating Procedures documents will be instrumental in training new employees and communicating the unique methods of your business.

One can just about mathematically prove that working on an evolving model committed to Best Practices and SOPs will produce more profits than a more random process.

Your ascent can be as follows: after careful study, you settle on one great idea and plan its future. Then write a business model, develop Best Practices to achieve your business model, and finally, write and keep up-to-date, specific procedures in order to operate each aspect of your business.

Anything that is not covered above is the meat of your business: creative employees who dynamically work with customers and solve problems. This, along with leveraging stakeholder feedback, will constantly enhance your Best Practices information base and improve your income.

As we see it, there are Four Main Strategies for achieving additional success:

(1) Delegate Tasks: The bigger and more profitable, the better it is for business. In this way, you can keep saying "yes" to all the great opportunities that you discover and pass them off to others who will help deliver the projects and their requisite profits.

(2) Build Efficiencies into all parts of your business. In this way, you can provide the same services as a larger corporation, but on a lower budget, and compete with those who previously

appeared untouchable. This can empower you to offer lower prices, too, if you choose.

(3) Learn More: When you know your products, the economics of your industry, and your sales prospects better than your wannabe competitors do, you will be able to make more deals faster at their expense.

(4) Work More: As you recall from Chapter 1, maxing out raw man-hours can provide exponential growth and tremendous value.

DON'T DENY BETTER OPPORTUNITIES

You have to be willing to analyze potential business improvements or you are in denial. Don't bury your head in the sand. If there is evidence of better methods of action for your business, then you need to understand and execute those new methods.

Quite frequently, entrepreneurs who may appear to be concerned about their business and personal profits are able to overlook or ignore mounds of Best Practices that are continuously being exposed by associates, industry leaders, the scholarly press, and others. Often pride and ego lead us to believe we already know it all, which gets in the way of rational, proactive decision-making.

If you are working smarter, you can work less to get the same results (or the same amount to get better results). Unless you are being stubborn, (even subconsciously) you can realize extra profits by employing Best Practices and pushing forward.

If there is too much on your plate and you can't proactively pursue and develop new ideas, at the very least, you should still do a cursory review of fresh business concepts when they cross your desk. With any available free time that you may have, study these ideas before dismissing or accepting them. Dismissing anything outright without even giving it a glance means you could be passing up many profitable deals or ideas.

It is all right if you do not fully pursue some good ideas or plans.

In fact, you are supposed to be looking at and rejecting many ideas in your active vetting process. But there is no reason you shouldn't give yourself at least a few minutes a day to look over any relevant, promising deals to determine whether they could enhance your arsenal of focused strategic business ideas and assets.

Keep in mind that one day down the road, you may want to be in another type of business and adopt an idea or two. If you start reviewing your options early, even in a rudimentary way, you can follow and understand the concept before some possible competitors. You could even place early strategic bets if you choose. Getting involved in good ideas sooner rather than later is more profitable.

You will always be pushing forward from status quo to profitability or backwards towards financial loss. You can't stand still because you are being measured based on moving targets (the performance results of your competitors). You have to be proactive just to stay even with the competition, and still, that won't get you very far.

For you to excel in business, you must understand how to turn all of your theoretical Best Practices into actual day-to-day strategic advantages. You can always create better operational tactics in a more assertive manner that will eventually wear the competition down and lead you towards the top position in your industry.

Document and replicate the successful activities of those who have come before you if they have delivered good results. You could attempt to take shortcuts, but they probably will not work, and they definitely have a lower likelihood of working compared to studying, documenting, and proactively pursuing Best Practices.

The friction, obstacles, and market conflict that you confront in your evolutionary business processes are signs of progress, not problems. Those with no friction are stagnant and ready for corporate slaughter, but a disruption of the status quo can potentially enhance the market, its presence, and its margins for everyone—with you in the lead.

Somebody out there is getting paid big money. If it's not you, then it's best that you imitate the leaders from your chosen industry and adopt their Best Practices to mix with your own.

Those who pay attention to and further develop the Best Practices that dominate their industries and follow through with each detail will always get the best results. Leveraging these compounded results over time can readily equate to wealth for you and your family if that is your goal.

Every time you fail to assertively take advantage of all opportunities and employ all Best Practices, you are essentially throwing cash right in the garbage (or even worse, into the hands of your competitors). This money is called Opportunity Cost.

Controlling opportunities requires a careful setting of priorities. An example would be if you spent 10 hours to make $100 when you could have chosen a better business option and spent 10 hours to make $200, then the Opportunity Cost is $100. You lost $100—the cost of making the wrong decision.

The opportunity to improve in all areas of business is always at hand if you pay attention. You should be willing to build or you are choosing to stick to a less profitable path by default.

One way to help you see your business in context is to envision the outcome you are looking for and then work your way backwards to identify and prioritize all the tasks it will take to get there (basically reverse engineering your future business). Someone has probably done something similar before and you can see what actions and characteristics led them towards success.

If you follow Best Practices, the only relative disadvantage you could have to your business peers is your original education and background. Those who were better educated or somehow raised better will always have a theoretical advantage for you to overcome. You may have to make up for lost time, but eventually, you can catch up to your competitors if you stay focused for an uninterrupted stretch.

DO ZERO-BASED BUDGETING OF THE MIND

When determining government appropriations for future years, some politicians recommend "zero-based budgeting." Nothing is sacred in this situation, and there are no programmatic entitlements to funds just because they were appropriated in a prior fiscal period.

Similarly, we believe companies are not entitled to do business the old way. Instead, you should be constantly checking to ensure the old way still makes sense and eliminate any commercial preconceptions in your mind; as a result, you can maintain an open mind and be prepared to change the way you think, like Warren Buffet, Steve Jobs, and Bill Gates tend to do.

Even if you are strongly attached to every aspect of your business, it couldn't hurt to consider what other options exist.

Although much of what you have learned in the past (particularly from your parents and your schooling) can be applied to your business, you have to be eager to let go of any ideas that no longer make good business sense. You need brain space for newer and better ideas; do not become stuck on the way things used to be or how you wish they were.

This beneficial brainwashing effect is what we call "zero-based budgeting of the mind." Take nothing for granted and re-examine what will really allow you to accomplish your goals. The details of your industry and your business are what they are and you must comprehend and accept them. In addition, you must also know the effects you can have on these details, and therefore, your market at large. The main thing holding businesspeople back is the failure to pay attention to real facts and details. Instead, they become stuck on false ideas about what will make them successful. Your mind is your only barrier to success; you can decide to break down that barrier anytime you choose.

"You are entitled to your own opinions, but not your own facts." If you become stuck on the wrong track, you could fail. Of course, using our methods, failure is not an option.

Similar to business leaders, military leaders are expected to make risky decisions every day during wartime to advance their cause. Every day is wartime in the business world, unless you are just playing the role of the victim of aggressive competitors. You are either a victim or a perpetrator in the economy (or the winner or loser of the war).

Some people become paralyzed with fear because of this responsibility and have a hard time moving forward aggressively. On the contrary, if you approach your opportunities with good information and know the approximate level of risk involved with each possible decision, then with that level of confidence, you need not hesitate.

When in business, you have to take calculated risks every day. As long as you understand the key risks and opportunities inherent in each deal, you can hedge by placing many bets. Presumably, if you do proper due diligence, they will all have a greater than average chance of going in your favor, and you will have safely spread your risk. Those who are hesitating, getting scared, or becoming paralyzed lose out on the opportunities at hand, and typical industry leaders are moving on to the next big thing.

GET FIRST MOVER ADVANTAGE

All songs are improvised in the beginning. The musicians who create and perform this original content generally earn more than imitators do.

Similarly, those who develop a company or invent an industry are likely to be paid more for a longer duration than those who are copying them. Certainly, you could successfully copy other people in business and improve on their products and services. But, to earn even more, it's better to be the first to operate within your niche and then to remain the best.

If possible, you should be the first player to enter your industry; the first to invent the products, services, and processes that make your industry tick; the first person with access to the best employees; and the first with the best marketing ideas.

Unfortunately, you can't have it all. Yet, as long as you are trying to get it all, you are on the right path. So go for it! Try to be first to enter new markets or niches.

You will move ahead if you are merely operating on par with your competitors. But if you can operate better than par overall AND are among the first to enter your markets, then you are more likely to capture a compounding "sustainable long-term advantage," which should become synonymous with a "perpetual profit stream."

Like your own company, your competitors are also always

moving either forward towards profitability or backwards towards financial loss. To the extent that your operations are similar, you will advance and decline at roughly the same rate as the competition. That's why you want to start first in your market and continuously push further ahead. Being first to market requires accessing and understanding information and then applying what you have learned quickly in many small, calculated risk trials.

Make sure that you are researching every angle relevant to your industry and operation. This includes reading every trade magazine, attending most of the conferences, regularly calling on all the major industry players to establish relationships, and so on. It only makes sense for you to have something to offer in return to those who share resources and information with you.

If you start out with sound business theory having thoroughly studied your market, your tests will have a much higher chance of positive results, indicative of a positive market opportunity. If you are paying attention to the trends in your industry of choice, you should know as much as anyone who has done similar preparation and more than anyone who has done less.

While it is usually better to be involved in the beginning of an industry's development, it isn't possible or preferable in every case. But you can still enter almost any small, mature industry if you want or a niche area that is surrounding it. Hesitation can be overcome with ample research, planning, and self-confidence.

It is great if you are fortunate enough to be the first person to think of a good business idea; although, you can't prove its worthiness without testing it. There is a certain element of risk involved due to the cost and time spent experimenting which can be avoided by borrowing the best ideas already in the public domain…and those 'best' ideas are all around you.

If you study what others are doing, you can discover a great business area that interests you and is generally profitable.

Apply that same model to another geographic market when possible since you are better off not trying to beat your competitors at their own game and in their own market until you are very polished.

Once you have stabilized this model in the new market by breaking even or matching ordinary industry profit levels, you can then begin to improve each of the parts independently while continuing to take the best new ideas from across your industry.

You can also accidentally be too early to a market if you are the inventor of the product or market niche, particularly if patents or safe secrets do not protect you. In this case, there might not be enough paying customers yet, or at least not enough to make a profit.

If your research uncovers a promising long-term business concept, then aggressive competitors could invest heavily in the market and potentially "blindside" you, creating a new industry paradigm. Conversely, you could persistently use your best ideas to get financing, secure attorneys, employees, patents, and so on to get the head start they have neglected.

Another type of business structure derived in Japan is called keiretsu. A keiretsu, sometimes called an "incubator" or "catalyst" in the US, is loosely translated as a family of affiliates or a business group with overlapping stakeholders and interests.

In a keiretsu, affiliate companies have purposely planned and created interlocking technologies, directorships, shareholders, and joint business ventures. The business that is carried out within a keiretsu group is not exclusive, yet they will generally look internally for services and human resources before considering outside resources—a "you scratch my back, I'll scratch yours" system, or a Web 2.0 style "old boys club," with girls, too.

A keiretsu group's synergy delivers extra power and profits

because the businesses proactively work together towards mutual success. The author of this guide is part of a loosely formed keiretsu where resources, talent, and technology are often shared to deliver innovative offerings across the Internet. In our case, companies such as Phone.com, SEO.com, Graphics.net, Skateboards.com, X3O, BrowserMedia, Yield Software and others often work closely together in a compatible long-term manner. Kleiner Perkins in Silicon Valley is famously profitable for its style of technology investment keiretsu.

EMBRACE NATURAL SELECTION

Business success mimics evolution. Cavemen, for instance, had to be efficient when they hunted for mates or food in order to preserve their genetic code through survival and reproduction. Indeed, self-preservation is the very essence of life.

The life expectancy for cavemen was around thirty years. If they were not effective at hunting, they would not be strong enough to fight their competitors for food and mates and would become extinct. Therefore, efficiency is a matter of survival. It may not be pretty, but natural selection works the same way in business as it does in nature, like it or not.

The act of successful customer prospecting, which is fundamental to business success, is predicated on business "promiscuity," which perfectly imitates mammalian promiscuity. You have to be willing to expose yourself continuously and risk rejection more than competitors to ultimately gain acceptance and reach your goals, whether it be a completed transaction or its biological counterpart, intercourse.

Video game competition is a modern example of natural selection. Gaming teaches kids hand-eye coordination and helps with their concentration, which are skills that can be used later in life for war, sports, hunting, and the like.

Interest in survival training is built into our genetic code in order to help us compete and evolve. Presumably, there are some rewards for being the best gamer, as there are for being the best caveman hunter, or possibly the best businessperson. In any case, they all follow the same basic precepts of natural selection and self-preservation, which is similar to Darwin's initial explanation in his classic work, The Origin of Species—a book that should be studied by all serious businesspeople.

Work and business are essentially competitions for market share. Granted, it may be a friendly competition at times, but ultimately, you are going head-to-head against others who want the same customers as you.

If you become operationally superior to your competitors, before long you will show that you have surpassed a break-even point. From here, you can endeavor to prove to the marketplace that your products are relatively better than your larger competitors' products.

At the next level, you will be as profitable as your competition on a marginal basis, and you can also achieve the same raw profits if you have created even higher margins due to super efficiency, sometimes even with lower overall revenues.

As illustrated, you are striving to be on par with the best profit producers after which you can continue your assault by operating ever more efficiently. This will result in higher profits for you per transaction and customer, and you could therefore make equal profits even with lower overall sales. Completing your tasks faster and being more aggressive will ultimately result in an enhanced evolutionary state for your firm at the expense of your competitors.

Even though you are trying to metaphorically "kill" your competitors, their ability to compete is merely what you need to destroy. You want to be an efficient and effective "hunter" to survive at the top of the food chain. Your weapon can be an endless stream of advantageous transactions.

Obviously, nobody wants any personal harm to come to the competition. Yet self-preservation and self-defense to try to kill them financially by "stealing" their market share is fundamental to business.

On the other hand, keep in mind that co-opetition, where companies simultaneously cooperate and compete with others in their industry, is the order of the day for fast moving, modern businesses. So being too abrasive towards your apparent competition could have side effects that prove to be detrimental when it comes time to working together, and it could even hurt your broader reputation.

Remember that he is your opponent or competitor, not a personal enemy. Ultimately, burning bridges can harm your bottom line and your morale. Certainly, be very aggressive in your market but draw the line at unacceptable, anti-competitive, or illegal behavior.

Evolution is the result of a series of mutation tests. You must adapt your processes in a competitive market by creating mutations from the baseline of what currently exists in that market or business. Understand the status quo and force evolutionary mutating processes to expose the methods that will work best for your business and against your competitors.

Small ideas that are tested and adopted serve as new mutations in a small company's biologic system. Unless there is an ailment, mutations in nature are only permanently adopted and replicated if they are genetic improvements. The more mutations tried, the more opportunity exists to discover which ideas prove to be genetic improvements: i.e., enhancements over the former version of the corporation. As you become more and more advanced, any non-evolving competitors will quickly become obsolete, victims of the process of natural selection.

Not only should you proactively test mutations by your actions, you should also attempt to force them into your thought process in a wide variety of ways to create possible opportunities to separate yourself from the pack. Break out of your comfort zone regularly.

One way to do so is to place yourself in mental or emotional situations that will allow you to view your dilemmas and opportunities under differing "mutated" lights. For example, reconsider an important business situation while on the beach, at the gym, at 3AM, while you are swimming, elated, or upset, in the snow, on vacation, at a concert, in church, in the woods, in an airplane, etc. Whatever ideas and information you believe you have stumbled on during these forced mutation sessions, compare and balance them against each other, as well as against other ideas that are vetted in more sobering settings, like the office.

Hence, the object is to get as many perspectives on your business issues as possible and pursue actual tests on those ideas that appear to be most relevant after the initial process. This method purposely mimics how mutations can arise and how they are advanced in nature.

So as you can see, the new ideas you adopt along the way should be added to your arsenal of Best Practices while replacing old ones where necessary. The wide variety of tests, ideas, and people that you require to succeed is akin to a large genetic pool for natural selection, so you can adopt the strongest characteristics from that pool in order to survive, thrive, and multiply. Those companies that are moving more slowly and not testing enough "DNA" combinations will become extinct, and the leaders will lead.

WELCOME TO HYPE THEORY

Take the double helix of a DNA strand. The two strands are dependent on each other in order for life to exist and DNA to replicate. The DNA's helix structure serves as a blueprint: one strand denotes faster evolving traits, like hair and eye color, while the other strand carries the stable genetic traits, like the formation of bones, lungs, and so on.

Fundamentally, business works in a similar way. You should have your baselines, like CPAs, lawyers, data systems, and so forth to allow stability in your business and processes, but you should be making mutations in your sales, marketing, PR, merchandising, dealmaking, recruiting, research and development, and other methods in order to evolve and beat your competitors. On one hand, your basic structure and DNA is protected, while on the other hand you are in radical, proactive mutation mode in order to figure out how to create additional wealth for your shareholders.

Likewise, life is a stable baseline that protects our art and us. Art helps mutate our minds and activities to envision the next generation of our lives until we ultimately make ourselves stronger and more appealing to others, which means we can compete better. The stability of rational people ensures that the radically evolving, mutating nature of art does not lead us too far astray but only improves us, just as mutating evolution provides the opportunity to improve an otherwise stable business.

Take a chicken and its eggs. While the chicken is the baseline, the egg has the opportunity to mutate in order to adapt stronger competitive characteristics, so the chicken's basic genetic stability ensures that the egg does not stray too far while trying to diversify and improve the chicken's genus.

We know that cash or salary makes employees feel comfortable and stable; however, since it's a sure thing, it doesn't make them terribly competitive. This is why stock options are often used as an incentive to motivate them to mutate into more effective, efficient, and ultimately, more profitable workers. However, with no salary component, most employees feel insecure and unstable. The two are mutually dependent to enable an optimized competitive evolutionary environment for your business, much like the double helix DNA structure, life and art, the chicken and its eggs, and other mutually dependent evolutionary models.

Based on the above, I crafted a business philosophy coined "Hype Theory." Hype Theory holds that two forces, hype and reality, follow the same patterns of natural selection discussed above, and they are mutually dependent on each other for optimal success. Hype and reality working in concert enable a powerful evolutionary force as does a DNA strand.

- ✓ ■ The Reality: you work hard every day on creative processes and products to make your clients happy.
- ✓ ■ The Hype: at the same time, you can project the proposed greatness of your future company to the press, your prospective clients, and others.
- ✓ You are simultaneously protected by your base reality (of excellent plans, products, employees, intellectual property, financing, and so forth) and can therefore safely project your hyped up confidence in the market, which is likely to appeal to new customers and help uncover a variety of potential opportunities that you are qualified to

leverage. Again, you are creating a self-fulfilling prophecy by projecting your real world confidence.

Here is our attempt at an equation to explain Hype Theory:

Life + Art = Nature + Nurture = Chicken + Egg = Cash + Stock = Reality + Hype

They all feed off their mate and are intrinsic to the other to create success. They engage in codependent, evolutionary, symbiotic, mutual self-preservation. One stabilizing force allows another force to radically explore options and adopt the best of them without destroying the sanctity or functionality of the base business. So to the extent that you hype and simultaneously believe in your own services, others will follow, which will advance your business just as the other parts of Hype Theory work together to guarantee successful evolution.

GAIN CONSENSUS

The more trusted professionals who tell you that an idea or plan is sound, the more likely it is to be true. While you should not make decisions based on "groupthink," or averages, or "management by committee," and while you absolutely can't be slowed down in your process, it is always helpful to consult others and take into account their opinions to discover if consensus is readily attainable.

Independently determine which deal options you believe are the best based on your own in-house research and concept development process. Then talk them through with key friends, consultants, and stakeholders.

If you have independent advisors with a broad range of knowledge and experience, and if those advisors are blessing your major business moves, then the plans will have a higher likelihood of success. If the advisors all reject your concept or proposal, then there is a greater possibility that it is, in fact, a dud.

If some advisors are in favor of your proposal and some are opposed, use your best judgment to navigate the gray area. You are best off evaluating all of the information and advice and then make an independent verdict. Maybe waiting a little longer, studying a little more, and chatting again with each advisor will uncover a clear answer. When trying to gain consensus on big decisions, it's best to have at least a trusted accountant, a lawyer, a few skilled businesspeople, a friend, and a relative run by it. Skip any "yes-men" (like your mom).

Dr. Dennis Mulumba

Gaining consensus on major business decisions doesn't shield you from any responsibility for the bad ones.

MASTER EFFICIENCY, LEVERAGE, AND SCALE

You can always produce more and be more efficient than you previously thought. Therefore, you must prepare your infrastructure early on if you aspire to grow. With greater scale, you can accomplish more with less effort, even though it will still take considerable work to achieve anything worthwhile.

The idea behind leverage is that as you amplify your success and money, the resources you control become even more of a draw to vendors as well as potential employees, partners, customers and investors. This means that each dollar at a larger company should go farther than the same dollar at a smaller company. The more resources you have, the more attractive you are to the business world.

You can create leverage, and with it, you will be in a position to extract better prices on products and services, find better candidates for job opportunities, and attract more demand from prospective customers. Leverage facilitates additional pricing power and even enables further discrimination in your choice of customers.

If you are too good at growing your business and you feel it's beginning to move too fast to maintain quality, then your prices can always be raised to new customers. In fact, the high demand for your services proves either you give great service, are too cheap, or are just a good overall value. In any case, this leaves you leverage for additional pricing discrimination. Another option would be to re-focus your marketing just on the most profitable niches you've tested, so less time and fewer dollars are spent in less profitable areas.

Over time, you can invest double the money and energy in the most profitable niches you're developing (double down) and dump the remainder. Alternately, you could keep all your niches fully operational, as long as the parts are compatible, and your investment dollars should go further.

Plan in advance for each task you undertake to be bankable, meaning it will lead to real profits within a reasonable period. Merely filling time by "faking it," or producing academically good yet unprofitable work rather than making serious, planned and measured financial accomplishments, will not help one reach his goals. Focus on analyzing the metrics that best represent key aspects of your corporate performance to guide you towards future Best Practices.

Your leverage should primarily be due to your provision of quality services and products. If you have something of value, people need to know about it so you can use this strategic positioning to your advantage.

For instance, West Coast Choppers (WCC) is a small custom motorcycle company with clients who are generally mega-millionaires. In this case, one would assume the clients, and not WCC, would have leverage in negotiations since they are wealthy and powerful. But in reality, the service and product quality from the WCC's shop is so high (and their customers know it) that they have leverage in every deal. As a result, they can extract ostensibly high prices and other favorable deal conditions from their customers.

They don't abuse their right to use leverage lest they lose it. If customers were to sense a pompous attitude or price gauging, the WCC brand could easily be diluted and lose hard earned leverage.

Providing quality services over time and promoting them accordingly creates additional service demands, which creates valuable leverage, and therefore, opportunities to appropriately scale your entity. Here is one simple example of how scale can work to the advantage of a business: if you were a real estate agent, you would discover that selling a hundred homes is more than a hundred times as profitable as selling one. The more homes you sell, the less time, energy, and money is consumed per transaction.

This same basic precept applies to almost any product or service: making 200 sales is not 20 times harder than making 10 sales. At some point, you hit sweet spots where successive transactions aren't proportionately more expensive to produce. Added up, these sweet spots show patterns that prove scale offers significantly advantageous financial opportunity (dollar for dollar; hour for hour) compared to chugging along on a steady course, at a low level, with light resources.

Taking a private company public generally invokes a public premium because of the public buyers' perception of the advantages of scale, and because there is substantially greater liquidity.

The public premium gets you a higher share value compared to a private company with the same amount of profits, revenues, and projects. So you see that added liquidity is yet another way scale provides companies with extra leverage, which means each additional dollar of profit will come with less effort.

The bigger you are, the more money you should make merely due to your size and the added efficiencies created by your size, assuming that bureaucracy doesn't paralyze your business like it does many large organizations.

Often, your competitors do not believe they can effectively scale their organizations. They conveniently think that their current size is their optimal size. In this case, your strategic advantages are for you to understand economies of scale better than the competition, believe you can effectively scale, and be willing to make an assertive try at it. Just as the rich get richer, the bigger companies with more scale, and therefore leverage, get what they need cheaper and faster. This leaves them at a perpetual advantage by effectively distancing themselves ever further from their mainstream competitors.

Don't forget that incompetence or wasted time in large or small businesses could readily reverse any strategic advantages that scale may offer.

In many cases, the mom-and-pop shops that are content with their productivity and profits are at perilous risk. The client relationships of most small businesses that appear to be sustainable, in reality, are potentially "ripe for picking" by more aggressive small businesspeople who are operating with more scale, efficient guerilla tactics, or lower operating costs. It is not fair; it is just business.

There are other ways to gain economies in your business besides becoming a larger company with more employees. These include replacing old technologies with newer ones, and sometimes hiring fewer people in favor of employing technologies that are more advanced. Cutting expenses and growing without incurring additional fixed costs will also result in bigger profit margins, which will be enhanced later by applying an "industry multiple" in order to assess the company's fair market value (FMV) for mergers and acquisitions. This is where the most money is likely to be gained.

OH, OH, DOMINO

To illustrate the main points made in this chapter, let's take a look at a real-life example of a company that rose to the top of the evolutionary business ladder, Domino's Pizza.

There are good reasons why Domino's is the leader in the pizza delivery industry. At one time, they were no different from the pizza shop around the corner or all the other little pizza shops in the country. But something propelled them to extreme riches and success.

Certainly, their pizza is not the best in the world. Domino's made it big because they wanted something more than the rest and they believed they could get it. The mom-and-pop pizza shops were not primarily concerned with corporate growth or personal riches.

Domino has worked the hardest and smartest. They hired the best help for their purposes, tested many different ideas, paid attention to all of the details, and used great accountants, lawyers, and marketing experts to grow safely and effectively. They chose to succeed at something bigger.

Domino's domination is the result of natural selection. The combination of fast, professional, and efficient services, combined with good pricing and food good enough to satisfy their target market, allowed them to win the evolutionary competition in the modern pizza industry.

Likewise, you can apply all of these theories to your own business, no matter what its size or offerings. Every company is a work in progress and it's up to you to pave the way to a leadership position in your service area. You can become the Domino's of your own niche if you choose.

SELL YOUR COMPANY

If you are successful, you will capture an ever-growing share of your market and its profits. Ideally, your financial charts will show your company's revenue and profit lines consistently climbing a slope without blips (down slopes), which would be perceived as weaknesses to the outside world.

If you have a track record showing that you've been able to handle sustained growth, then there is a reasonable chance for a prospective buyer to expect that trend to continue, and he will jump at the opportunity to bid for your company.

In other words, if your business methods make sense and you grow profits quarter over quarter, then you can likely be bought for a fair present value, and the buyer can capture the future value of your company's growth. Ideally, these buyers would be strategic buyers who, on top of the cash, could offer you profitable synergistic relationships with their other business assets, ostensibly making one plus one equal three, where each party shares in the accretive margin created by the deal. On the other hand, strictly financial buyers might just see a good deal and want to buy it, with or without a sound forward strategy of their own creation or compatible assets. However, if they will pay you enough to meet your needs, you may want to take it anyway. In addition, they are likely to pretend they are actually strategic buyers. In reality, the most likely possibility would be a buyer who has a little bit of each of these tendencies.

Unfortunately, some players working on deals, be it attorneys, accountants, owners, buyers, consultants, or employees, are hampered by incompetence or egotism. In fact, this is the most common scenario that causes otherwise good deals to cave. It is even more prevalent than the huge issue of sellers who use questionable math. Do not be surprised if they are often the same people. Companies with leaders who have noticeable ego issues should be handled carefully, if you choose to deal with them at all.

If you are a potential company seller, many prospective company buyers and middlemen will try to engage you in a mating game where they woo you with displays of affection to encourage you to sign a contract with them. This dance will include a combination of facts and nonsense being thrown at you. Not to mention that you will be barraged with questions which are meant to elicit what likely should remain confidential information until a deal is certain.

Furthermore, some seemingly friendly people who present themselves as prospective buyers might just be gathering information in bad faith as part of building their internal "Best Practices" arsenal, but at your expense.

Until you have studied the buyers, their reputations and whatever offers are forthcoming, take the corporate mating overtures with a grain of salt. This is a key area where experts on your team, such as attorneys and CPAs, will prove to be invaluable.

Any information you want to disclose should be prepared in advance so you aren't caught with your guard down. It's also a good idea to know in advance what type of deal you might accept, if any.

If you don't want to sell your company for a fair market value, then don't waste your time and money by working with people interested in mergers and acquisitions. They won't pay more than what it is worth, and you won't sell for less.

The most common, conservative model a buyer is likely to use to estimate a target corporation's current value is discounting its estimated future cash flows back to what they would be worth today, given their expected profit margins over time, while taking into account expected interest rates and competing opportunities for higher yield. This old-school Benjamin Graham/Warren Buffett-type methodology is based on real economics instead of what are often pipe dreams of young entrepreneurs.

This exercise will be used as a guidepost for their offer, which is likely to have many interrelated parts, generally including some at-risk components, like stock options and "earn outs."

There are many factors a buyer will consider in determining your "estimated future cash flow," which you, too, must consider for your business "narrative," to create the intended perception. They will be interested in your longevity, intellectual property, resumes and bios, customer lists and contracts, debts, service liabilities and opportunities, leases, hard assets, non-compete and proprietary invention agreements for staff, the sanctity of your "books," and a variety of other objective and subjective measurements in their "due diligence" process.

Ideally, if you personally like the people (which would be considered one of the "social" aspects of a deal, as opposed to one of the factual financial aspects) and you believe that they represent the best potential buyer of your company, then you might give their offer extra consideration beyond its price.

However, keep in mind that the attitudes the buyers present might not be genuine, and the people with the most money can afford to put on the nicest presentations, often without being questioned by seemingly lower level businesspersons.

If your own job is going to survive past a buyout or merger, you will definitely want to make sure that you are working with the right people. With that in mind, spend a good amount of time with the prospective buyers to see if your social values and communication mannerisms are compatible.

Your evaluation of the buyers should take into account intangibles like courtesy and stress level during negotiations and beyond. But don't let their visits become intrusions and distract you from your daily business processes, or your company could become worth less during that period when you are trying to "flip it."

A Letter of Intent (LOI), or term sheet, which proposes some of the key deal terms in a professional manner, may not be "bankable" but could be a good start to a longer term, more serious deal and relationship. However, you ultimately need bona fide, fully executed, binding contracts (Operating Agreements/ Private Placement Memoranda (PPMs)/Subscription Agreements), which have been blessed by your legal counsel, before you should feel comfortable that your merger and acquisition attempts were a success.

A common "package" of buyout terms may include any combination of cash, stock, and performance-based incentives, including "earn-outs," which are tied to future revenues, profits, or events, as opposed to just stock price.

Overall, you want to understand the total value of the package you are being offered from buyers—and don't believe it until you see it in writing. Each piece of their offer should be balanced with the others until you feel comfortable with your overall impression of what's being offered.

If you get fewer shares of stock, you should get more cash or other incentives. The overall package, including the aforementioned social aspects of the deal, is what you need to weigh against any other possible offers. If there are no other offers, you can keep growing the company independently and try to sell it again later, or you can choose to take the best of what you are presently being offered.

Most of the intrinsic value in companies is usually created in its formative years. So, if you are productive in the early years of corporate evolution and less productive or interested in more mature operations, you could earn more money by starting and selling many different early-stage companies. On the other hand, switching could have consequences, too: like paying extra taxes, possibly needing to learn a new business, and definitely having to re-orientate yourself to new players in new markets which will likely result in lost leverage.

Another potential problem is that you could have a non-compete agreement, which would prevent you from competing with your former employer, the company to whom you sold out, and thus, require you to start in a completely new industry or territory.

Should you employ this early-stage sell strategy, the best bet to employ would be to focus on emerging industries, even though they are the most risky. By definition, emerging business niches don't have entrenched players. Generally, you can compete head-to-head with any industry entrant at your level of sophistication and wealth in emerging markets.

But if the game is decided by heavy up-front capital expenditures, then the person or company with the most cash will likely win. However, small emerging industries, which are not terribly capital-intensive, are open to everyone.

When you choose to sell your company, you will need to decide if your company is big enough to require an outside business broker to create merger and acquisition opportunities or if a great lawyer and accountant will suffice with your own leadership. Are people already making fair, unsolicited offers, or is it going to be a much more difficult process requiring more calendar or clock time and some professional help?

There is a common method used in mergers and acquisitions that can help determine the fair market value of your company. FMV is the only price for which you can sell out; nobody wants to be in on a deal where fairness is not taken into account.

The idea is to create an equation where you can plug in your company's "numbers" to arrive at FMV. Generally, a buyer who wants to disclose his valuation methods refers to a multiple of revenues or profits. This should equate to what they claim to be the FMV of your company.

Often, industry players create commonly known multiples for companies who have similar histories, financial results, and corporate structures. Irrespective of marketmakers' attempts to homogenize companies, once you review any of them in detail, you'll find that all companies and deals are truly unique, and therefore, require dynamic human and industry research, abstract insight, and a diligent work effort to discern the information you will need to make or receive a merger offer. For a small Internet company, a popular multiple is eight years of the company's profits (an 8X multiple). If you succeed in selling your company for a multiple of eight times your annual profits, you get the earnings of eight years hard labor (assuming no growth) in one payment (or however many payments you agree to). In addition, you can compound all that money for the eight years you would have otherwise been working, while saving all the opportunity cost and time to perform another mission of equal or greater importance or profitability.

This same company may have a 25% profit margin, and therefore, their revenue would be four times as high, making their "multiple to revenues" equal 2x to go with the 8x "multiple to profits."

Selling your company may save you years of work if the buyer delivers you those same years of expected profits from your operations but years in advance. On the other hand, if you don't successfully make your transaction, you could end up investing a lot of time and money in the sale-making process for negative returns.

Whatever your goals, you should run a business "as usual" during any sale process. It is vital to build long-term value in your company, whether you choose to sell it eventually or not. Buyers only want to buy assertive companies with bright prospects and current growth, not short-term schemes.

KAIZEN: A JAPANESE WAY TO APPROACH BEST PRACTICES

"Kaizen" is a Japanese approach to the workplace that has proven to be a famously effective Best Practices strategy with companies like Toyota and Sony, among others. "Kai" is defined as continuous improvement while "Zen," a more familiar term, is loosely translated as for the better or "good." Therefore, kaizen is to make "continuous improvements for the good."

Kaizen follows three principles: 1) process and results;

2) systemic thinking (the big picture); and

3) non-blaming, because to blame is counterproductive and wasteful in practice.

When kaizen is applied as a daily process, everyone in the company is involved, from the CEO and management team to your employees. The purpose of kaizen in the workplace is to eliminate the waste (or "muda" in Japanese) that is produced by your company, like waste in poor time management, inner office clutter, and other inefficient methods, while freeing other opportunities. Some companies hold a "Kaizen Event" where managers and employees work together to fine-tune and revise the current standards. Once a more efficient and superior system is achieved, it is then standardized and integrated into current policies, rules, and Standard Operating Procedures

(SOPs).

When you implement kaizen into the workplace, you should aspire to make changes to your current operating standards by breaking down each process in detail, monitoring the results, and then making adjustments accordingly ("If it ain't broke, Do fix it").

Your management team should ensure that the current SOPs are being followed. Management must "go and see" operations, or MBWO (management by walking around), in order to achieve efficient operations and take corrective actions when required. That is the only way they can fully understand their current business climate and make educated adjustments.

The Toyota Corporation is renowned for its production system, The Toyota Production System, and its principles, The 14 Principles of the Toyota Way. Kaizen is the leading philosophy behind their efficient and productive systems and methods. Jeffrey Liker is the author of The Toyota Way: 14 Management Principles from the World's Greatest Manufacturer. He writes, "The main ideas are to base management decisions on a philosophical sense of purpose and think long-term, to have a process for solving problems, to add value to the organization by developing its people, and to recognize that continuously solving root problems drives organizational learning."

The Toyota Way has been called "a system designed to provide the tools for people to continually improve their work." If you are not striving for constant improvements within your company, your business is not evolving, and neither are your employees.

Everyone on your team should be included in creating and attaining a well-organized, competent, and economical system. The benefits of empowering your employees create yet another virtuous cycle. It enriches the workplace and the work experience by allowing members of your company to excel and "bring out their best."

If your team creates more efficient processes, you will gain faster lead times and keep wages down. All of this is to help keep you ahead of your competition. You can then add those new moneymaking activities to your Best Practices and SOP arsenals for redistribution and reinforcement.

The methods that can help you successfully manage and organize the workplace in kaizen are called "the 5 S's", or "good housekeeping," as referred to by others. They are set in place with the intention to simplify the work environment.

The 5S's are loosely translated as:

Seiri (Tidiness): Unused and unneeded items are cleared out (this applies to your contact management system, too). Keeping your data organized, refreshed, properly labeled, and backed up are efficient ways for you and your staff to locate data as needed. The benefits of applying Seiri are a safer and tidier environment, less time wasted when searching for items, fewer hazards, less clutter to interfere with productive work space, and additional space from cleared out items. And possibly more brain space, too.

Seiton (Orderliness): "A place for everything, and everything in its place." Seiton focuses on the need for an orderly workplace to promote workflow. Conversely, seitan is a vegetarian meat substitute, and satan is...well, forget it.

Seiso (Cleanliness): Indicates the need to keep the workplace clean and neat daily. The key point is that maintaining cleanliness should be part of everyday work—not an occasional activity initiated just when things get too messy.

Seiketsu (Standardization): When the first three are set in place, they are then standardized. Create the rules, and then regulate them. Since it is easy to fall into old habits, this sets easy-to-follow standards and develops structure and conformity.

Shitsuke (Sustenance): This refers to educating and maintaining standards. Once the previous 4S's have been established, they become the new way to operate. Maintain the system and continue to improve it.

BEST PRACTICES FOR YOUR TEAM

The following list of Best Practices is a guideline to get your employees organized and in the right direction. We invite you to use these ideas with your staff and expand on them as needed.

1. Pay attention to details. Always return phone calls, spell properly in client communications, pass on messages, clear all problems to the client's satisfaction, keep your paperwork and computer files orderly, discuss timely opportunities/concerns with others, keep updated to-do lists, and other specific responsibilities. If a client or prospect requires information, then make sure the fax, email, and other communications that you send them are professional.

2. Offices should be clean and orderly and you should encourage random and scheduled client visits. Everything should have a prescribed home: paperwork, disks, cables, and shared hard drive files. Every teammate requires easy secure access to whatever resources they may need.

3. Be patient and polite to all clients and prospects but move to quality conclusions quickly. Ideas must become realities rapidly. No entrenched ideas or positions should hold you back. Be open to new and better ways of operating.

4. Be entirely customer-focused. Be committed to providing the best solutions for your clients' needs without sacrificing the bottom line. Constantly communicate with existing and

prospective clients regarding many services and issues. Staff from multiple departments should make calls to clients to "check-in" on their satisfaction and offer additional service. Talk and meet with clients more often and study their needs.

5. 85% of your time should be spent doing projects, sales, and customer service. The remaining 15% should be improving customer service to enable more sales while offering your present clients better value.

6. Employees should have the feeling that their organization is superior to competitors so they can happily express that to others. In any area where a person doesn't believe this to be the case, he should take action to change it and discuss it with others at departmental meetings.

7. Read and share relevant articles and books on your specialty; study the official technical specifications guiding the details of your industry; learn from other employees; try new products; apply and achieve mastery of the freshest technologies; and make learning a treasured component of each position.

8. Push your sales and marketing program hard so you can:

i. remain at the top of your business peer group;

ii. take more training courses;

iii. gain market share;

iv. do more stuff as a group like parties, dinners, and trade shows;

v. buy new stuff;

vi. get raises and bonuses; and

vii. defy remaining naysayers.

CHAPTER 4:
Modern Methods of Business Domination

GLOBALIZATION

The modern world is an immense place, and business people are constantly underestimating the size of global markets and the value of each share. Many worldwide markets are growing faster than corresponding markets in the United States; therefore, your share of one of these foreign niche markets could have greater growth potential than a share of an equally valuable American market today. Working internationally could give you better long-term opportunities if you choose well.

Despite great international opportunities, do not underestimate the limitless fantastic opportunities in portions of the U.S. and anywhere on-line.

Ever-evolving globalization makes world commerce much easier. Businesspeople in all countries can readily communicate with U.S. market players and vice-versa via telephones, Internet, SMS/Text Messaging, FedEx, translators, jet planes, and so on. If your competitors don't know how to go global and you do, then you will likely gain market share at their expense.

With globalization, you can easily have your German employees engineer products for your Canadian market while using a Florida distribution center, Indian call center, and Swiss bank.

COMMUNICATING TODAY

Everyone in the world is either on your team, a competitor, a customer, or a referral prospect. In other words, no one is irrelevant in today's global economy. However, a more targeted and often local market is where most of your dollars should be invested, despite your desire to be globally appealing.

When you don't have critical face-time with your clients and prospects, keep the e-mails and phone calls flowing. Also, return calls promptly and politely to those who could possibly help you make money in one way or the other.

General business and community contacts produce goodwill and quality business leads over time, even if not short-term cash. When you initially do business with someone, they will appreciate your professionalism and be happy to work with you under a future and favorable relationship, or refer you to other prospects. Being accessible, reliable, and proactive will pay off. Goodwill throughout your social and business communities will work to your advantage.

You can always politely refuse any deal that may not appear beneficial while maintaining your profit margins and your dignity. Conversely, not effectively responding to businesspeople and offers could lead to missed opportunities and damage your reputation.

Nowadays, there is no excuse for poor communication. We have speed-of-light e-mail, voicemail, cell phones, Palm Pilots, laptops, and Blackberries—all in a single device if you want. You can literally contact almost anyone who isn't hiding, almost anywhere, at almost any time. Your only excuse would be a lack of motivation.

Many of your prospects and contacts may not be adequately responsive, but this reality should only increase your volume of attempted communications rather than decrease them. As a result, you will receive more data on what is effective, which you can continue to reinforce, as always, against the interests of your competitors.

If you are continuously receiving poor results, even with a quality feedback loop from your tests, then you need even more communications and contacts in order to make enough money to survive and set yourself up for future advancement.

Again, nobody is offering a quick path to wealth. But even if an easy path doesn't exist, a rational and difficult route will still work.

KEEPING YOUR WORD

Staying true to your word is extraordinarily important, and many people don't do it or they try to fake it. Those people lose credibility and leave you, the competitor, in the driver's seat. No matter how tough of a businessperson you appear to be, how many people you fire, or how many people want your customers, one thing is for sure: if you always speak clearly and honestly, you will gain respect in your industry over time from coworkers, customers, competitors, and vendors.

Personal credibility is essential if you aspire to be a true leader. Tell it like it is, unless it's proprietary—in which case, don't say a thing. This way, over time, you will have access to the people and the deals you will need to be successful.

Leave storytelling to Hollywood and leave business to the businesspeople. If someone is going to work twelve hours a day on a real career, living in a fantasy world, making up stories, or not following up on promises will be of no benefit to them. That is only a way to bankruptcy.

CO-OPETITION

As stated in the previous chapter, co-opetition is the concept of simultaneously engaging in competition and co-operation within your market. This can potentially enhance the broader market for everyone.

Wikipedia defines co-opetition as "the concept of limited cooperation between competitors, usually arising in rapidly changing industries where companies are compelled to work together."

"Examples of co-opetition include Apple and Microsoft building closer ties on software development, and the cooperation between Peugeot and Toyota to develop a new city car for Europe in 2005."

Small companies can more readily benefit from co-opetition since the deals can be simple, and small partners can grow faster than large ones due to lethargy and bureaucracy created by size.

As long as you disclose anything that could be perceived as a conflict of interest to your partners in advance, and cover yourself properly with a nondisclosure agreement, then you can and should safely attempt to engage in co-opetition, including merger and acquisition-related activities.

USE DATA WISELY

In every line of business, you can leverage data to extract extra value. In fact, data manipulation could possibly become one of your most fundamental business processes.

For example, if you were to become a real estate investor, you could study market trends with help from computer database queries. When you have collected all available data on the properties sold in your target region, you could easily import that information into a variety of databases, and then merge it with the standard Multiple Listing Service (MLS) data set, which is the most fundamental and up-to-date data that real estate brokers and agents rely on to conduct commerce.

Next, you could assign various field names (like neighborhood, average income, growth rate of community, recent sale prices in neighborhood, school quality, distance to subway, highway and shopping, and so forth) to classifications of data and thereby effectively store and manage the characteristics of each record.

Then you can browse and run queries on the data to start discovering market trends and inefficiencies that haven't been fully exploited by your entrenched competitors. If you've discovered statistical anomalies in your market that others have overlooked, or failed to leverage appropriately, your business will have an advantage to exploit these opportunities.

It could be of benefit if the category of data you require doesn't exist currently in the marketplace. You could have an extra strategic advantage by developing and controlling the data set and being a "first mover" in the market niche that you have been studying. If the data already exists where you can easily find areas of low hanging fruit to exploit, you need to start using it in a faster, more effective way than the competition.

Understanding information about your clients and prospective clients is critical. So document and study the data on their spending habits, demographic and business information, subjective notes, and so on over a long period to gain valuable insight and act accordingly.

Keeping in mind how essential data is to your business, the ways that you store data are equally important. Nowadays, a filing cabinet will not suffice for all your documents since most of them are probably electronic, or will be as technologies develop.

You'll need a very simple, flexible, and scalable system with secure access for your authorized staff. If possible, you should try to have all documents stored electronically and make sure new documents and data are "backed up" daily in a separate, secure location.

It's important that you can instantly find all of the documents that you use to manage your business, which includes any contracts and Best Practices documents. Furthermore, your paper and electronic documents should all be named in the same type of syntax or manner, and possibly alphanumerically coded if you produce a particularly high volume.

Giving your documents long names with applicable keywords will likely make them easier to find when sought on-line or in print. There is free software called X1 that you should use to immediately find any data on your hard drive.

Cryptic document naming would make it hard to find what you are seeking. Thus, naming should be done using plain words. Likewise, subject lines in e-mails and memos should include the topic and project at issue, so your system is organized and information is easy to store, sort, and find for future use.

Another effective medium of distributing documentation is through Adobe PDF where you can practically create an exact copy of any document, fax, graphic representation, and the like. This can then be easily e-mailed around and printed in its original form.

We recommend you also use an on-line fax service, such as eFax and Phone.com fax service, so all of your faxes can be stored on-line and in e-mail format.

New telecommunications technologies incorporating Voice over Internet Protocol (VoIP) into a virtual office, which stores all of your messages and other telecom related information, will be critical in the near future. To simplify telecom management, try Phone.com.

Yet another important strategy in gathering data is to keep notepads and small digital recorders handy in your car, bedroom, or anywhere else you may be so you can document any ideas, Best Practices, or to-do items that you think of when you are not near your computer.

You should keep all of your ideas and information documented and at hand for further review. At the fast pace you will be working, you can't attempt to memorize everything that crosses your plate. So find a way to get it in text, audio, video, database, CRM, and so forth before it slips your mind.

For e-commerce purchases, Overstock.com is an easy, user-friendly, and cost effective way to get what you need. EBay, Amazon, Staples.com, Costco.com, Buy.com, and plenty of other well-respected sources can also get electronics and office products to your door overnight so you can improve your productivity the next day.

REPORTING AND DOCUMENTATION

Good reporting is critical in order to manage and display your business data; it must be timely and accurate.

Monthly reports need to be thoroughly analyzed with assertive corrective actions taken when required.

Business projections need constant updating.

Accounts receivable need to be assertively pursued.

Data from QuickBooks or other financial management systems need to be accurate, detailed, and up-to-date.

Ordinary monthly financial statements need to be delivered, like a Balance Sheet, Profit/Loss (Income) Statement, and Cash Flow Report.

Financial systems need to be integrated as much as possible (billable hours, purchase orders, inventory, and the like).

Read up on Accounting101 and/or hire a bookkeeper with the requisite skills.

Being disorganized or having poor documentation and filing procedures can cause tremendous problems for any business. Most businesses are not totally optimized in this regard; therefore, you can gain yet another profitable strategic advantage over your competitors through good organizational documentation and reporting.

CONTROL INTELLECTUAL PROPERTY

In addition to regular business information, you need to understand and keep an inventoried portfolio of all your company's Intellectual Property (IP). IP refers to a legal entitlement that sometimes attaches to the expressed form of an idea, or to some other intangible subject matter.

This legal entitlement generally enables its holder to exercise exclusive rights of use in relation to the subject matter of the IP. The term intellectual property reflects the idea that the subject matter is the "product of the mind or the intellect," and its IP rights may be protected by law in the same way as any other form of property. Intellectual property can also apply to lyrics and poems.

All of your intellectual property should have value to your firm, as long as you have proactively developed and protected it to the best of your ability.

If you develop software, for example, the code itself may be considered your intellectual property and could have components whose processes may qualify for a patent.

A patent is "a grant made by a government that confers upon the creator of an invention the sole right to make, use, and sell that invention for a set period."

Whether your software is patentable or not, any computer software or text document can be copyrighted. The definition of copyright is "the legal right granted to an author, composer, playwright, publisher, or distributor to exclusive publication, production, sale, or distribution of a literary, musical, dramatic, or artistic work." If you wrote a book, your copyright is intellectual property.

If your company name is unique and not descriptive of the services you offer, then it likely qualifies for trademark protection (TM). A trademark is "a name, symbol, or other device identifying a product, officially registered and legally restricted to the use of the owner or manufacturer."1 If your logo is unique, it qualifies for trademark protection, too.

In general, intellectual property attorneys have cozy relationships with their colleagues at the US Patent and Trademark Office (USPTO), even though conceptually that could become a costly conflict of interest. They will unfortunately make sure many successive filings are required in order to ensure that your patent or trademark is successfully registered, if it can be registered at all.

It is crucial that all IP paperwork is carefully organized and safeguarded. The registration process through lawyers is generally unreasonably expensive, regardless of the risk that the filing ultimately might not be approved.

The IP attorneys don't take jobs on contingency or have caps on their bills; as such, they generally make the process as long, confusing, and multi-part as possible while jacking up fees along the way. Still, IP protection is not a process that should be skipped merely in the interest of saving money. Your branding and intellectual property protection is critical and will be profitable in the long run. If you can find a way to save money in the process, more power to you—but don't skip or delay it under any circumstances, or you could lose the massive value that is potentially right at your fingertips.

The earlier you attempt to control and protect your intellectual property, the more likely you are to be effective, and at a lower cost with less hassle. This is yet another case where one of our favorite and most critical concepts in growing a profitable business applies: "Break the calendar."

Also, if you fail to properly control your IP, then the sale price of your company will be adversely affected should you attempt to sell it.

GET IT IN (SIMPLE) WRITING

We like to emphasize "simple" because it is critical not to become bogged down with endless paperwork, bureaucracy, and attorneys. This is too expensive, too time-consuming, and rarely adds significant value to deals. The bigger the deal, the more overhead you may consume—but don't do so for small change.

Paperwork is an infamously tedious part of business. In fact, parties frequently procrastinate in completing paperwork to seal a deal, even when it has been negotiated ad nauseum. Usually, what you think is merely paperwork ultimately requires further negotiations that are nice in principle, but contentious and time-consuming as they become more detailed.

Without paperwork up front, you wouldn't have a business plan, or documented Standard Operational Procedures, employment offers, web service contracts, and so on.

In addition, you can't buy costly products and services without well-documented, signed term sheets or formal agreements.

Paperwork should be quick and efficient, not backlogged. Again, you'll need to hire a good lawyer and someone who can help write or edit your documents to get you through these stages of business.

If a vendor charges by the hour, you should have her quote a range of expected hours in advance along with the details of what is to be accomplished upon completion. Also, try to pay as little as possible up front so you maintain some leverage in the transaction and protect your cash flow.

Some people seem to think they are immune from "getting it in writing," and certainly, nobody should be. It is amazing how frequently people expect others to agree to something of financial significance without producing paperwork that explains the details and its exact cost.

Paperwork is also necessary to protect yourself legally and financially. Often vendors prefer to leave things vague until it is time for you to pay for their products or services. Even though the price will no longer be vague, how it got so high and how you'll be able to pay for it probably will be!

HARNESS INTERNET POWER

In today's digital world, you can use the Internet for an even greater share of your business needs at an ever-decreasing cost. The power of the Internet is critical to succeed in your evolving business.

In order to do business outside of your immediate geographic service area, the Internet is an indispensable tool. Therefore, you should try your hardest to set up as many business functions as possible that take advantage of Internet-connected services.

Having a good website is one of the best marketing tools you can develop for your business—if you do it right. The days where you could say, "It's too hard to get a website," "It's too expensive to get a new website," or "I don't need a new website" are over. You must have a comprehensive, good-looking, functional, and user-friendly website if you want to manage a proactive, modern corporation, and it should be updated regularly with fresh information.

At the very least, your site should have a good domain name, a memorable logo, the products and services you offer, your corporate history, and your contact information (phone, fax, e-mail, IM, a special Phone.com number, LinkedIn, Facebook, Twitter, and so forth).

After that, try to provide as many of your real business services as possible with e-commerce through your website.

Hire experts to assist in planning and deploying your Internet functionality and design since the development process can only be done professionally if it's your own specialty. Website and brand development companies like Graphics.net, Browser-Media, and others offer professional level services that exceed these standards.

Do not forget updated spam filters, virus software, and backups for your PCs and network connected servers. Don't put real e-mail addresses on your website,. Use forms or temporary e-mail addresses that are deleted.

THE FUTURE OF THE INTERNET AND TECHNOLOGY

Looking forward, the world will have cheaper laptops, iPods, iPhones, Blackberries, Sidekicks, iTVs, Skype and Phone.com phones, PDAs, HDTVs, digital radios, RFID-enabled devices, GPS receivers, Wi-Fi devices, SMS and Bluetooth thingamajigs, other handheld, integrated multimedia social devices, and a wealth of additional automotive and specialized electronics to try.

All of them will be connected wirelessly and through fiber optic cable and routers to cheap storage space via powerful processors, leveraging TCP/IP routing technology, speaking to state of the art data systems in a grid flush with real-time social, business, shopping, and entertainment connections.

Billions of people will be able to do anything they can imagine electronically, whenever they want, from wherever they want —quickly and inexpensively. Exponentially more ones and zeros will be traversing the planet ultimately delivering games, TV, voice, music, SMS, video, podcasts, chat, videochat, blogs, email, search, and so on. They will be using display technologies like HTML, Java, PHP, RubyOnRails, Flash, AJAX, Flex, RSS, PDF, etc., via open application programming interfaces called "APIs" using XML-type standards that will talk to MySQL and Oracle databases, Linux and NT-based operating systems and the like. All of this will occur while conducting serious e-commerce and delivering managers real-time actionable analytics.

The point is that no matter what you call it—shopping, e-commerce, flash, VoIP, television, audio, Podcast, blog, message board, wiki, chat, IRC, HTML, JSP—it's all ultimately just the modern display of ones and zeros upon the future device of your choice.

WHAT ARE DOMAIN NAMES & WHY DO I NEED SOME?

The following primer on the importance of domains is adopted from BuyDomains.com.

A domain name is a company's unique identifier on the Internet. Yet, Internet computers only know how to transmit information with Internet protocol (IP) numbers: for example, 128.256.37.18.

However, IP numbers are confusing to consumers and cannot be branded easily.

The Domain Name System (DNS) was created as a solution to translate these difficult to remember IP numbers, associated with your company's web and e-mail hosting services, into your own easy to remember, brandable domain names, to help your customers find and remember your services. The same unique domain name can be used as the root of a company's Web address and/or their e-mail addresses.

The format for a corporate Web address in the United States is usually "http://www.mycompany.com/". It does not have to begin with "www," but it has become standard over time and is easy to remember. An e-mail address is generally myidentity@mycompany.com, with most common ways of expressing your identity looking like flast@mycompany.com, firstlast@mycompany.com, first.last@mycompany.com, fml@mycompany.com, or first@mycompany.com (at smaller companies). In this digital age, it is not a good idea to use another company's domain name in your Internet dealings. For example, the e-mail addresses company@aol.com or company@yahoo.com does not properly identify your unique business. Using such domains in your communications implies that your company might not be Internet-savvy or implies that you want to be anonymous. Or it could imply that you are an employee of AOL or Yahoo or whatever domain with which you have associated yourself.

More importantly, it doesn't help you to reinforce and market your unique company name. Besides, it looks unprofessional and can be difficult typing in a Web address with such a format as www.myisp.com/mycompany.

Having a domain name that clearly relates to your company, like smithcompany.com, joespizza.com, softwaretraining.com, or rockconcerts.com, will resolve these issues and allow you to establish a strong and professional brand on the Internet.

THE IMPORTANCE OF SEO

The purpose of having a website is so people can find and read your work. Search engine optimization (SEO) is the process where your site is analyzed and then modified to increase its rank on search engines like Google, Microsoft, and Yahoo. Your website's ranking on a key word search is essential to directing it. Proper SEO ensures that your website will be readily, professionally indexed by the search engines.

In a keyword search, search engines in particular send out what are called web crawlers, also known as spiders, or robots (bots). "Web crawlers are mainly used to create a copy of all the visited pages for later processing by a search engine that will index the downloaded pages to provide fast searches. Crawlers can also be used for automating maintenance tasks on a Web site, such as checking links or validating HTML code."[2]

Companies can invest tens of thousands of dollars on a website, but if it has not been properly optimized for the search engines, then it will not be indexed or found. And if your website is not indexed, then most of your web development investment will be spent in vain because web crawlers will simply bypass your site in most pertinent keyword searches. If you are not investing in good search engine optimization for your company's website, not only will you lose exposure via web traffic, you will also lose money. SEO ensures accessibility to the search engines.

In order to have success operating on the Web, hiring professionals to optimize the experience is vital for businesses and nonprofits alike. Not only will proper optimization improve your ranking on the search engines, your company will also benefit from the practically free advertising value from the extra "eyeballs" that a higher-ranking website attracts.

You should be just as competitive when optimizing your company's website as you are in your day-to-day business activities. Statistics show that internet users rarely, if at all, go beyond the third page when doing a key word search. Your site rank is essential to directing traffic inward and making it a "sticky" experience for consumers because your competitors are literally just a click away.

Understanding the importance of search engine optimization, Google has created a set of guidelines to consider.

Design and content guidelines:

- ✓ Make a site with a clear hierarchy and text links. Every page should be reachable from at least one static text link.
- ✓ Offer a site map to your users with links that point to the important parts of your site. If the site map is larger than 100 or so links, you may want to break the site map into separate pages.
- ✓ Create a useful, information-rich site and write pages that clearly and accurately describe your content.
- ✓ Think about the words users would type to find your pages, and make sure that your site actually includes those words within it.
- ✓ Try to use text instead of images to display important names, content, or links. The Google crawler doesn't recognize text contained in images.
- ✓ Make sure that your TITLE and ALT tags are descriptive and accurate.
- ✓ Check for broken links and correct HTML.

- ✓ If you decide to use dynamic pages (i.e., the URL contains a "?" character), be aware that not every search engine spider crawls dynamic pages as well as static pages. It helps to keep the parameters short and the number of them few.
- ✓ Keep the links on a given page to a reasonable number (fewer than 100).

The authors of this text co-own and operate a consultancy called SEO.com and an SaaS (software as a service) software company called Yield Software that are renowned leaders in search engine optimization.

FINDING WHAT YOU NEED ONLINE

You need to know how to access the information you need online as quickly and efficiently as possible. "Boolean" is one way to bolster your Internet wisdom. This silly word represents a very easy and powerful method of finding what you need on the Internet.

For example, merely adding quote marks ("....."), or (+) and (-) signs in front of some of the words in a Google search will dramatically improve your search results, thereby providing access to many of the most valuable and pertinent on-line resources in seconds, and at no cost.

After you retrieve good quality search results, you should select the most relevant links to "drill down" and then visually scan the results. If you read the domain/URL that comes up under each search result link before you click it, there will be hints on the relevance of the information and its source. Generally, longer URLs are more likely to link to "ad-centric," useless content than shorter URLs, which often have good quality content.

Review many potential information sources from the results of your Boolean Internet search. As a result, you will have a better chance at finding those most pertinent. Drill down on the most promising links to read, print out, bookmark, keep notes on, and upon which to generally focus.

CHAPTER 5:
Make Dollars Use Sense

In your early years, you could attempt to have a relatively hectic lifestyle in order to earn more money and equity, to save up for a more relaxed lifestyle down the road. It is natural for younger, single people to decide to endure more risk and higher work-related stress for rewards that are potentially far in the future.

While you must earn enough to pay for your family's home, food, clothing, education, and healthcare, most additional purchases are discretionary.

It is up to you if you really want to compete at the highest levels and acquire more discretionary income, or if you would be content with having a "good job" and a relatively relaxed lifestyle. Regardless of the path you choose, only you can surmise which balance is most appropriate for your own family's needs.

We believe that it is more profitable to compress as much labor as possible into a shortened timeline to thereby create the maximum efficiency and overwhelm your market. Working more may not necessarily be better for you personally, but it is more profitable than a slower evolving business. For us, the main point in maximizing one's discretionary income is to apply this leverage to charitable works and to spend more retirement time with your family on the beach, or on your own dream of choice.

HEDGE RISK

When going into business, you are essentially reviewing and strategizing your options and then placing your bets. By placing more high quality bets, you are hedging your risk and limiting your potential losses.

Diversification of your investments is a tried and true way to protect yourself. On the other hand, it limits your upside potential, too, since, by definition, all of your money will not be exclusively in the most profitable investment; instead, it will be hedged (or balanced) across a number of deals for safety's sake. In theory, this is one reason why mutual funds might be safer than individual securities but will also have a smaller upside potential. Conceptually, the more volatile an asset is, the greater its upside.

You can't wait for a risk-free deal to invest in because there is none! And if there were, it would only promise a miniscule return, no better than a bond.

Not betting consistently on the best deals you can find, and instead, trying to time your market entries and exits at the expense of fundamental research and conservative investing, is unlikely to work unless you are extremely gifted.

Nothing is guaranteed for the market leaders or their followers. As long as you know what you are doing, taking risks can actually be less dangerous than not taking them. Playing it safe instead of proactively conducting business might not be so safe at all.

Hedging bets is the same as hedging risks. While any one risk might be too risky, hedging across many smaller deals can create balance, and hopefully, less risk, if each bet is educated.

BUT BE DECISIVE WHILE HEDGING

People become paralyzed with decision-making because of the risk involved. But if you approach opportunities with good information, and therefore, know the approximate risk of each decision, then you need not hesitate.

If you are in business, then you are in the business of taking calculated risks. Make sure you understand the key risks and opportunities on each possible deal. If you do proper research, your hedged bets will have a greater than average chance of working out in your favor, proving you have safely spread your risk.

Naturally, when you do this "better-than-average" research, you will have a "better-than-average" chance of profiting more than your less studied, wannabe competitors will.

However, if you have only one asset in your portfolio, you'd be at a greater risk of that sole deal failing. Hedging will prevent wild swings, either up or down, in your overall net worth.

Those who hesitate, become scared, or feel paralyzed, will lose the best and most time-sensitive opportunities at hand, including compounding growth early. Typical industry deal leaders will keep pushing on through to the next big thing as expected.

PURCHASING STRATEGY

When purchasing big-ticket products or services for your company (or even hiring people), the initial pool of prospective vendors should consist of notable industry leaders plus other vendors who have been referred to you personally by business associates or personal connections.

If you have an uneasy feeling, or you don't fully trust any of the possible vendors, then you should immediately eliminate them from your prospect list regardless of their pricing and services. Additionally, you should always be direct and polite to all the potential vendors who have to be eliminated.

When you are done with your basic research and analysis, you should have at least three candidates left to consider further business discussions and negotiations, ultimately ending in offers from some. Look carefully at your final candidate's portfolios of work, their array of products, and related reviews. You should also find as much information as possible about your targets on the Internet.

Hopefully, you will know people in common who can provide an additional level of reference, and even security, since both of your reputations are at greater risk if you have a broad or closely connected personal network. You may be able to call other clients who are listed as references, but keep in mind that some may be prone to give biased reviews because they may receive discounts or quid pro quo treatment or feel obligated to give a good reference due to personal relationships. Nevertheless, if you ask good questions and you are given objective references, then you can glean useful information for your purchasing and hiring needs.

During the vendor vetting process, there should be many opportunities for you to communicate with each prospective candidate. If his or her assistant is doing most of the e-mailing and phone discussions on behalf of your preferred principal, you can assume that is how the relationship would play out in the future. Also, if he or she is unprofessional, or doesn't return your calls or e-mails as expected, then you can assume it would only get worse after you sign a service contract.

Typically, vendors are on their best behavior before a deal is consummated. So, if you don't like the treatment you get when they are on their best behavior, then you will hate the treatment you get after you are under contract. It's best to eliminate these sorts of people from your process before you become dependent on their services.

Once you have cleared out all the objectionable vendors, you will be lucky to meet your target of three good-faith offers from trustworthy candidates. At that point, you are also hoping or pushing for the offers to be comparable (apples to apples).

As you continue to review the proposed project's documentation and your interactions with the vendors, you may be able to decide which ones you favor even prior to having thoroughly reviewed their pricing.

But if you are really comparing apples to apples, and all the vendors and offer formats are essentially the same, and even further, you equally like all the vendor interactions, then price and payment terms are all that matters. The bottom line is the bottom line if all offers provide the same quality for the same services. So if you like several of the vendors, and their offers are practically incomparable, then your decision will be harder to make.

In reality, hiring vendors is not so clear cut and not necessarily at your unilateral discretion. For example, if you live in the northeastern United States, you probably had to suffer from the notoriously hideous phone services of Verizon and their predecessors Bell Atlantic, Nynex, etc. since they are the monopoly providers in most areas.

Those businesses that absolutely depend on phone services to survive are in a pickle. They have to pay whatever outrageous charges the monopolistic providers throw at them, or they will lose their services and could go out of business. Moreover, they have to accept minimal and poor quality customer service since the incentive to provide quality services is eliminated in monopolistic enterprises.

The same issue exists with Comcast Cable Television, another example of terrible and traditionally monopolistic services in the northeastern US.

With no incentives to improve, monopoly providers can be expected to give consistently bad service. In these two cases, weak pseudo-competitors exist today, but they are still severely handicapped by legacy issues, such as being forced to lease their competitor's ancient systems' infrastructures at non-negotiable prices set by politically and financially influenced utility boards.

In many other cases, there are only a few products and service providers for the items you require or desire, so you are beholden to the limited market whether you like it or not. If you are uncomfortable with the corner of the market where you have been boxed in, your best bet is to try to break the popular paradigm. Mix up your marketplace by constantly finding and creating alternative products and services to differentiate yourself from your competitors. This fundamental business strategy could create extra profit margin for your business while baffling the competitors.

Fortunately, a high proportion of deals, whether large or

small, only require you to review the pricing since you often know exactly what you want and have many commodity-like vendors from which to compare and select.

Once you have made a firm commitment in writing to your vendor of choice, you cannot gain any advantage by paying them late or withholding funds. You ultimately must pay your bills, so you might as well pay on time to avoid establishing two potentially fatal business sins: a bad reputation and bad credit.

Many people try to establish deal leverage or try to get an underhanded credit float by paying bills late. This approach will backfire, is a waste of time, and proves you are not paying attention to the critical tasks your time requires. There is no reason to upset vendors and force them to hold you in disdain for paying them late. If you need a loan, get one from a lender, or ask the vendor if they will provide special terms or financing.

As the leader of a company, you get to do all the hard work. Negotiating with vendors can be one of the most confusing tasks ahead of you because sometimes you don't know what a fair price is, and you can't tell if the person you are speaking to is being completely honest about all the details, or has kept any important information hidden.

Whether the spokesperson for the vendor is putting on an act or not, you might not understand why there is apparent disgust in his attitude if you reject his rate quote or overall offering. Would it be because his offer to you was truly fair in the first place, or because the salesperson is just pretending that you are being unreasonable? You must educate yourself on what price is fair before you come to the negotiating table in case the seller is trying to unreasonably "squeeze" you.

Any uneducated demands you make to the vendor are likely to be unfair in the first place. If there were a set market price, as in a commodities market, there would be practically nothing to negotiate.

But just because you find yourself negotiating a deal, doesn't necessarily mean there is an easy way to establish a fair contract price. In many cases, there is no correct price, and any negotiating position you take can readily be questioned by the other party. So if the other party produces apparent facts to justify his pricing, make sure that his information is 100% true, and the methodology and "facts" he used to justify his pricing can be well-substantiated before you rely on any of it for your own decision-making. In any case, make sure you have solid facts and can logically explain why the price and deal terms you wish to offer are fair.

Purchasing services is much like building a collection of your favorite CDs from scratch. You should take a broad look at the musical offerings from every genre that suits your interests and denote the discs you think are most promising.

Maybe you note bands because you've heard them play, or because they are from a regional hotbed of music, or because they are known as a musical pioneer in their field.

Next, you can take a sampling of the music available from those artists by listening to sound clips. As you listen, you can jot down the names, songs, and albums that you like most and remove any of the selections from contention that you don't like.

After final review and contemplation, you can purchase your final selections, and then the next thing you know, you have new music to enjoy based on a simple and sound vetting process, which might give you ideas for yet another set of music purchases.

When you buy services for your company, you should essentially go through that same process. You scan the names and basic information of potential service providers who might meet your needs based on references, reputation, or research. You then select the ones that look most promising based on your prearranged criteria. From there, conduct as much due diligence on each selection as possible, including apples-to-apples price comparisons.

Ultimately, you should do a thorough job of reviewing all pertinent options and then make rational, proactive, expeditious purchasing decisions.

Once you have easy access to product and service information and notes from a multitude of sources, you need to cleanse and think about the data on hand. Ultimately, you can make decisions and take bids from vendors who can fill in pieces of your business plan.

If you have three options as mentioned, you will find that you are buffered because if one doesn't work out for any reason, which is often the case, there are two others from which you can choose. With three options in your pocket, you can market your own services more aggressively knowing you have support, and use this leverage to gently pressure the service providers to provide what you need, when you need it, at a fair price.

PRICE IT RIGHT

Don't price products or services using round numbers. Odd prices may appear as though even more thought went into your decisions. In this way, prospective clients may subconsciously believe the prices you choose are "correct," and they may act accordingly. This phenomenon is intended to create less friction between consumers' wallets and your cash register.

Wal-Mart at www.wal-mart.com, Phone.com at www.phone.com, and DomainMarket.com at domainmarket.com are good examples of places that often sell products with strange looking prices that may end with "88," instead of the more common "99" or "00."

While round numbers seem honest and customers might find a price of $.99 to be sneaky, using $.88 is a way of getting near the next higher increment without actually marking the price up to the next round number.

The authors believe that "88" sounds good, looks good, is somewhat unique, doesn't risk offending people, and is simple yet appears to have required some thought or process. While the efficacy of creative pricing is debatable, it's easy to do and is unlikely to have negative effects.

NEGOTIATE WITH THE BEST

Most situations that require negotiating relate to staff issues, deals with vendors, deals with partners or investors, or sales to customers. Everyone has his or her own conscious and subconscious negotiating methods and agendas that go with their life experiences, personalities, and business skills.

We think that you, personally, should always be the one who proposes the framework for deals. You want to prove that you are motivated, organized, and confident, and that you can put together a deal on your own terms.

Come up with big ideas and offers that make economic sense and figure out how to explain them professionally in writing. Practice a lot, ask around, and read on the Internet and in the library about how to develop quality proposals. Also, at LinkedIn, you can easily find people to help you develop winning proposals.

One successful method and outlook in your negotiations is to be clear and direct from the start about which terms you may ultimately be willing to accept. This proves you have previously educated yourself on the issues, and you know what to expect throughout the process. Confidence adds value to your side of the negotiation and is likely to make the other party more confident themselves, which means the deal is more likely to close.

If the other party is receptive to your initial overall proposition, then most of your negotiations should be over the smaller details. If your proposal is not accepted, you will have saved yourself valuable time. Haggling over small points is irrelevant if the broader proposal is being rejected. In the case of rejection, it's likely to be an opposing party acting in good faith that will recommend alternative deal terms; as a result, it gives you the opportunity to accept them or to be firm, honest, and polite with your rejection.

Being direct saves time and helps keep you honest which provides multiple benefits. The only downside is that you are "playing your cards" publicly, so your responses may be predictable, and possibly weaken your negotiating position.

Rational parties may differ, but we believe in being direct and open as early as possible in your deal-making. This will get you where you are going faster, and with less friction.

MAKE LOTS OF DEALS

Doing deals in general may be the most profitable use of your time, as long as you are dealing in areas that you understand well. If you are trying to hedge your risks across many business opportunities and you have established an "edge" in deal-making by getting more and better information faster and promoting your "win-win" ideas, then you may find that seeking and closing new deals is more profitable than operating any one project.

Presumably, you have been developing innovative products and services since the inception of your business, and are performing your marketing, advertising, and overall brand-building processes.

Hopefully, this work is running fairly well. In any event, you need to focus on the general concept of "closing deals" to make more money, faster. Every time any type of business agrees to your price, and your lawyers subsequently produce good paperwork, you have a deal.

The same is true every time you sell a product. Generally, the bigger your deals, the better off you will be, and the more deals you complete, the more profitable each deal will be.

If you can manage each individual transaction without a significant increase in fixed costs, you can end up with a company that possibly has high fixed costs but low marginal costs—in other words, a scalable operation.

In addition, it's always beneficial to be the one who has the most legal power backing up deal negotiations. Lawyers can control the heavy paper flow that potential deals create and legally protect you from terms that could bite you in the end. Good lawyers will also provide valuable advice during each stage of your deal-making.

Keep in mind these important strategies below when you are preparing to make deals:

1. Clarify to the opposing parties that your commitment is to your shareholders.

2. After counterparts ask for concessions, make sure that's all. Then explain to them the concessions they should be prepared to make in return.

3. Be accessible, so the right people can find you when necessary. But don't just wait around for others to search you out. Make deal offers persistently based on the best ideas you have developed, if you can find qualified targets.

4. Make sure a wide range of options exist in deal terms so you don't lock your prospective partner into a "no" decision. Put them in "yes mode" for easy items, and then you can go in for the "kill," the main deal.

5. Go for large deals, even if the numbers occasionally turn out to be unrealistic. It's good practice for other deals when you will be able to get "big fish" and favorable terms.

6. The more time you and your business counterparts invest in researching a deal, the more likely it is to eventually close. With that said, if you lose calendar time, you may lose the intended cumulative effects of the deal in the normal course of our rapidly changing economy and fickle consumer base.

7. Be sparing in praising your vendors' services until after any deal on the table is closed. Always be honest in your evaluation of vendors once your service contract is in place.

8. Don't agree to any one specific detail until you feel you understand and agree how it is supposed to fit within the framework of an entire package.

9. Trying to pay the absolute lowest price to vendors may backfire and lead to a failed transaction or substandard service. For exceptional services, you should be looking for a low, yet fair, price.

10. Be relaxed in negotiations, or you will give off a sense of fear that may put off the other side.

11. While you should never allow yourself to be "beaten down," you are often expected to negotiate and compromise. If you don't want to do so, then politely move on to the next deal.

12. Don't compete or negotiate on price alone. Add valuable incentives.

13. Aim for exclusivity in your contracts to lock out your competitors.

As you see, making good deals will require a variety of skills and a lot of motivation. You need to be prepared to do whatever it takes.

CLOSE YOUR DEALS

There is a lot of money out there that is trading hands, and you get to compete for your share. The best way you can prepare for this is to complete your education and training, then put in long hours and gain on-the-job experience. Along the way, you will learn what to look for in a good contract and how to ensure all the terms you need exist like a good termination clause, an agreement stating your employees are not to compete with you or steal your secrets (A Noncompete and Proprietary Inventions Agreement respectively), and so on.

The relatively small details in every negotiation are less important than finalizing a deal overall, and ultimately getting paid, so don't let miniscule points keep you from closing the deal.

The bottom line is always in the math. If the math works and you are happy with the personalities of the opposing parties, you can't be scared to take on a project. Having said that, if other parties do not accept your math, the only leverage you have is to walk away. Therefore, you must be willing to walk with no personal attachment to any deal. A reserved disposition will help you make better business decisions without emotional baggage or confusion. Decide where your boundaries are and stick to them.

When you are purchasing from a vendor for the first time, and you believe your account is or will be one of their largest or best, then it's appropriate to ask for what's called most favored nation (MFN) status in your contracts. MFN will ensure that other customers (possibly including your competitors) are not getting better pricing, and that if they do in the future, you would be entitled to the same.

Deal-making is a lot like playing poker. Your hand represents your leverage, or lack thereof. Interestingly, in poker, your competitors cannot tell what leverage you have unless you have cards face up on the table. You pretend to have leverage by bluffing; in business, you can try the same. Yet, if someone calls your bluff and you cannot produce, you will have destroyed some of your credibility.

In poker, your competitors have to play directly against you since it's a zero sum game. Conversely, in business, both you and the competition can actually create a larger market for everyone to share, even while you are competing head-to-head in the existing market.

Another helpful analogy can be seen in billiards. Playing nine-ball is a cutthroat game. Namely, all the hard work in sinking balls one through eight is for naught unless you successfully sink the nine-ball, i.e., close the deal. You can sink the first eight balls yourself and play a fantastic game. But despite all of your successful efforts, just one good shot from your competitor when on the nine-ball will seal the deal in his favor.

Similarly, in business, it doesn't really matter how well you play throughout the game unless you win, get paid, or close the deal. All your hard work could generate a good reputation and good business leads for you; however, to truly be successful, you have to complete whatever you are working on at the top of your game—just like in nine-ball.

FINANCE THE RIGHT WAY

One should not get rich from a successful business financing experience unless the capital was being solicited from investors in bad faith. The only way you can get rich is from the profits generated from the effective application of the capital you raise.

It is shocking how many people in the "dot-com era" raised large amounts of capital to operate their vague, mathematically questionable ideas. Some "business leaders" ended up with easy, luxurious lifestyles as a result of raising a lot of capital. They would pay themselves in salary or bonuses, sell their own stock shares prior to their company reaching profitability, buy services from their "friends'" companies but finance them internally, or surreptitiously buy billions of dollars of services from their pals who would reciprocate—all to add revenue and hype for their Wall Street IPO appearances.

Nevertheless, what they failed to recognize, or possibly care about, is that sometimes they had done nothing of any value for their shareholders or customers. In fact, the opposite was often happening. Good money was going into companies to theoretically serve as a seed investment in order to develop a quality service platform, but instead, it indirectly went to finance the lifestyles of the recipients.

After having managed a successful and profitable operation, selling out your interests is an entirely different story from raising investment capital. Selling a long-term company with accelerating profits should indeed make you wealthy and enhance your lifestyle significantly. But one should not get rich from seed capital, as what used to occur frequently in the early years of Internet frenzy.

Another mistake is gloating over financing. Instead, it should be a wake up call to signal that you have a lot more responsibility in applying the extra capital effectively. The best bet for companies to use capital properly is for the capital that they consume to have been generated internally in the first place. In this way, they will appreciate the value of each dollar.

There are only two realistic ways to make extra money: earn it or inherit it. Since regular, hard-working folks generally don't come into inheritance, the most accessible way for them to earn significant cash is by eventually owning part of a business.

A small company raising a lot of capital is analogous to a young person inheriting a lot of money. Those who inherit money are less apt to effectively manage and appreciate it. They often have trouble managing easy money, and therefore, tend to spend in frivolous or irresponsible ways, i.e., invest and protect it poorly.

In contrast, those who didn't inherit a thing but earned the same amount are much more likely to have a successful money management experience. When you are dealing with the money that you've raised to start your business, always be sure to approach it as a hard-earned sum used in only the most appropriate ways.

TALK MONEY

People tend to be uncomfortable talking about money, or they may become offended by those who are money-centric. But guess what? Business is about money. So if you aren't talking about money, then you are being negligent. In fact, for clarity and good financial sense, just about every business conversation you have should be framed within the context of "money" or "making money."

You should be talking about whether or not your ideas are profitable or if they fit in with your strategy that was designed for maximum cash flow. Or you could talk about whether something is fairly priced or if it can be negotiated downward. Also, your talk could focus on whether an opportunity is a method of saving money by building evolutionary efficiencies into your business processes. Finally, you must wonder if the opportunity cost is too high for any particular business deal, and therefore, predictive of a loss of investment value.

In your personal life, you might not want to talk about money; in business, all you should be talking about is money. Possibly, you may want to be politically correct and explain to people why it is "all you care about."

Some examples of "money talk" may include: "It is my fiduciary duty to my shareholders"; "It is the reason why I am here"; "It is the reason the business was formed"; "It is how all of our families get fed"; "It is how I am going to retire"; and "It is how I will be able to do charitable works to help others."

These are among the many great excuses to be talking about

money during business hours.

When your attorney and broker calls you, make sure you are talking about money, too, including whether or not they are earning their fees.

People who you have to "shake down" may get upset. At least they will know where you are coming from every time you speak. If you leave your intentions vague, your results might be correspondingly vague.

The only exception is when you have to be discreet during certain business negotiations with the party on the other side of the table; in which case, you should keep the math close to your vest.

For example, if you have ideas and predictions for a part of your industry that your competitors might have somehow missed, you would not want to disclose this information, leading them to believe their own company has additional value, or directing them towards that opportunity.

In courting rituals relating to mergers and acquisitions, company buyers speak a lot about synergy, relationships, products, future, culture, and the like. We recommend you re-focus the conversation and talk about the math instead.

CHAPTER 6:
Pick Pumped up People

Next to the cold hard numbers that represent your profitability, the most important factors in any business are the people. Aligning yourself with the most favorable partners, hiring the right employees, retaining the best contractors, and maintaining all of those relationships simultaneously to the best of your ability are all crucial to your overall success.

Learning when it is time to let any less-than-effective, risky, or difficult stakeholders go is equally important. Your goal is to have the right number of the right people who are properly motivated and organized at each point of your corporate ascent.

PICK PARTNERS

You have to decide who you want your business partners to be, if anyone.

Some say, "don't do business with friends or family," which makes sense because all the stress in business could harm personal relationships. Conversely, who else can you trust with money and important decisions if not your family or friends? There is no right answer to this dilemma. Whether or not you choose to partner with family and friends, the best bet is to have partners with great track records, and preferably deep pockets, and/or extensive skills to bring to the table.

One way to avoid having family and friends as business associates is to be part of a network where you will get exposure to potential partners for business deals. You may discover prospective partners when doing the informal personal network building that is necessary for your marketing and other business purposes.

There are many ways to expose yourself so you can meet the right types of people to try to partner with for your new business: join associations, groups, Chambers of Commerce, country clubs, gyms in affluent areas, on-line special interest groups, and so on.

If possible, partners should have many personal references, and you should feel a sense of compatibility and trust. The longer you've known someone, the more qualified you are to consider them for a partnership.

If you can finance your small company without partners, then you can keep all the profits for yourself, as long as you can handle all the risk yourself. If you have the confidence required to succeed, then the risk is lower than it would be otherwise.

Also, take into consideration whether you'd prefer to own half of a business or a whole business half the size. Realistically, you want to own more than 51% of any company that you operate because owning more than half of a business leaves you with final control over the decisions, unless you have special covenants that specify otherwise in your shareholder operating agreement.

Of course, you still need to have the self-confidence that we mentioned in the first chapter, or you are better off working for someone else. In that case, your bosses are likely to dictate how much, if any, stock you will get. They will avoid letting you get to 51%, to say the least.

HUMAN RESOURCES: TRAIN, DELEGATE, MICROMANAGE

For a business leader who follows the aggressive strategies outlined here, letting go of partial control of the company will probably be difficult. In reality, however, a company where only one person handles the difficult details cannot grow to be very profitable. The profit margin may be high, but with a low revenue base, it won't spin off enough cash to meet your needs. A leader has to practice delegating on a daily basis, as difficult as that may be.

One of your main business strategies, irrespective of the industry in which you compete, should be to test many relatively inexpensive business ideas quickly. The ones that pass your tests can be reinforced and taken to the next level. Herein is a great opportunity to begin scaling your operation by hiring and training associates to oversee every unique business unit or project, as you should have studied and standardized many of your processes, and prepared training programs in advance.

After the training process, you need to supervise and review your managers and their progress. Over time, they should become mini-profit centers unto themselves and train others below them, as you have trained them.

In this way, you are developing scale to your organization and being paid for more work than you could ever possibly do on your own, as you are personally earning a portion of the profits that are generated from the hard labor of all your associate employees and those they hire. And since they, too, should get paid well, they will be happy to keep producing for themselves and you while further propagating your company's strategy.

Delegating tasks to well-trained subordinates and holding them accountable is your best bet in gaining the scale required to dominate each market niche, but that doesn't mean there is no micromanagement going on from above.

First of all, employees find it convenient to label almost any managerial intervention in a derogatory way as "micromanaging." But don't get sucked into the negativity that this term may imply.

The job of subordinates is to pursue corporate goals by participating in their development at the direction of their supervisors, not negatively questioning or criticizing their "superiors." This mandate includes the necessity for employees to be nimble and to be prepared to shift directions whenever current market data and momentum suggests it's time. While you may be on the same team as your boss, he is held accountable to shareholders, and therefore, has to make the final decisions.

So if your boss wants to review the fine points of your corporate initiatives, it is his right—more importantly, his duty— to understand the details of the business and re-direct efforts whenever, and however, he deems appropriate.

If this is labeled micromanaging, so be it. Successful companies delegate and depend on as many employees as necessary to manage and evolve every business segment independently, and to the best of their abilities. But at the same time, they have leaders who elicit information from their ecosystem that form the basis to make fast, educated decisions that can't always be perfect.

It may sound like a paradox to have a business that both

delegates and micromanages, but it is a matter of the areas to which each is applied and the degree to which it is done.

Before you hire new staff, do the math: if you are trying to decide whether you can hire five new people or not, consider how much extra revenue they could bring in to your operation and if it will be profitable.

So if you have five new people who each bring in $300,000 per year, you will then have an additional $1.5 million in revenue, which is almost certainly profitable overall, and therefore, worth their cost in salaries.

As much as we love employees, the real goal is for you to create as many automated processes as possible to mix in with your hyper-efficient, super-hard workers. Therefore, you would require fewer employees to manage the more automated systems, and everyone would benefit from splitting a bigger profit pie. (Again, nobody said this was going to be easy.)

While we may try to break this process down piece by piece, the overriding point is to work hard, have confidence, and test lots of ideas—try to get scale, leverage, and efficiency in order to raise your revenues and profit margins.

With enough financial growth year after year, and the beating down of your competitors, you will have millions of dollars and be ready for charity work in no time.

There is a well-known saying that goes "Hire the best, develop the rest." It's important to hire the smartest people so they are in fact trainable. Some of the most effective managers only hire a tiny percentage of job applicants to ensure that they get the cream of the crop.

Once you have hired the best people, make sure that you are supportive and mature when reprimanding, not angry. On average, punishment is counterproductive, so be careful when you are forced to reprimand those who aren't following your best plans and practices.

It is also important to provide clear job descriptions at the beginning of the process as a means to reduce turnover. Starting with a higher quality employee base will go a long way when you begin the continuous process of delegating responsibilities.

If a person doesn't really like their job or their pay, it's pointless to waste time training them unless it's already clear that they are moving in the right direction. The person who is being delegated the responsibilities really needs to "take ownership" of his tasks in order to make the delegation process worthwhile.

When you are training new employees, try to use real-life case studies and scenarios that they will deal with on a day-to-day basis. Also, consider sending the employees who interact with the public to a Dale Carnegie sales training course or even Toastmasters. To train is to learn; that is why it must be a daily process among your employees and for you, especially if you hope to train others.

INCENTIVIZE EVERYONE

Additionally, you should always make sure all of your teammates (co-stakeholders) are properly incentivized to work hard and get ahead. Contractors, business partners, industry partners, and the like should feel that they are in the same financial boat as you and each other; as a result, they will work better and harder for you and with you. So, if they perform at an outstanding level, and that makes your company evolve better and faster, then it makes sense for them to get extra pay.

In fact, you need your teammates to aspire to be high producers from the start, so encouraging them with financial incentives is often the most appropriate way to get the results that you require. There are many ways to motivate someone, but the bottom line is to always give deserving parties extra money for outstanding performance.

Often employees feel that they deserve extra pay, regardless of your interpretation of their performance level. While you believe their base pay is fair for the expected high level of work, they think they deserve more even before the incentive plan is slated to kick in.

Get used to it; everyone always thinks that more is needed. Explain your point of view so people understand what an incentive program is supposed to do for the company and the program recipients. If the program is vague or unrealistic, it will not serve its purpose.

The best choices for incentive-based programs include stock options, phantom stock options (which pay the same amount as real options but are easier to establish and have different management procedures), cash bonuses based on revenue, cash based on profit, cash based on sales volume, or cash based on hitting any other targets that you decide are reasonable.

One way or another, it's important to encourage people to hit specific benchmarks by offering them rewards for doing so.

Of course, you always reserve the right to award additional, unexpected bonuses to employees who have performed above and beyond the ordinary call of duty.

Unless you keep and disclose a reliable record of what other incentive recipients have received in the past, your new incentive recipients might have a hard time understanding what it takes to hit their maximum reward.

Oftentimes, even you cannot be sure what the result of incentive plans will be, and you may accidentally pay the person more, or less, than you've anticipated.

Your best bet is to choose the most predictable type of incentive plan: one that truly maps the amount of benefit to be paid to performance level and more than what is expected in the normal course of business.

You want all the stakeholders to realize the same thing you realize: working harder, smarter, and more efficiently has financial benefits.

BUILD YOUR TEAM

If you surround yourself with the best people, they will deliver the best results, for which you ultimately will get partial credit (and cash for that matter). Your focus needs to be on how to build the best team possible. First, seek out partners and employees on your own, and then, as your company grows, hire a great Human Resources (HR) person or team to find those people for you.

Carefully think through each position. Document what you want each position to accomplish and what sort of person would best fit. Then spread a wide net with the purpose of capturing the most viable prospects. This net should include an e-mail to your personal network, ads on your web site, and listings at web sites for job seekers (use FaceBook, LinkedIn, Monster.com, WashingtonPost.com and CraigsList.org, for example). Also, consider headhunters, newspapers, and local publications. And don't forget to promote from within because using already existing staff whenever possible will work best for everyone.

A virtual team can be effective for many types of projects, too, which could be considered "telecommuting", although, not all projects are appropriate for telecommuting. The bigger question is whether you are willing to personally direct the day-to-day actions and manage the hours of an at-home worker or not. One big issue is that they can frequently become sidetracked on side projects and family matters when they work from home. Another is there are many times they risk looking unprofessional, or miss out on professional networking, team building, water cooler chit chat, socio-business interactions, and the like.

If you don't want them as your employee or as a liability, consider hiring them as an independent contractor. This can possibly save you on taxes, benefits, and other expenses. Also, at-home employees may not be on the clock forty plus hours a week, so you won't necessarily be responsible for their full-time employment expenses, like the reimbursements for excessive fuel costs or lost hours in traffic.

Hire the people you think you need, but be careful because you have to be responsible for funding all your decisions. If you want to fund something or someone at a high level, then there must be a proven or provable payout cycle for you to become cash flow positive. It could be a fatal mistake to incur too much debt or otherwise put your company at risk.

The national debt is our government representatives' way of getting their cake and eating it, too. Government expense overages come from unfunded mandates, just like hiring people you can't afford.

Hiring good people must be done, but it has to include a careful funding process and be part of a seemingly profitable business model.

DON'T PLAY CORPORATE POLITICS

Corporate politics are a waste of time. Instead, people must let their work performance speak for itself. Trying to knock down people on your team is in bad taste, even if you feel they deserve it. If you are spending too much time thinking or talking about others on your team, then more than likely you are not properly focused.

You are on the same team as your co-workers and employees, and when combined, the results are all that matter. Your profits are not dependent on your title, the titles of your coworkers, or one's ability to direct another. As a technicality, or for practical management purposes, it may be necessary to have a hierarchy and titles, but this should not be an excuse for internal power plays. Delivering results is a team responsibility; certainly bureaucratic, political nonsense will not be helpful in your pursuit for success.

If someone is poisoned by corporate politics, then you can't tell if they are transmitting genuine information or useless, tainted information, which if relied upon, will be counterproductive. This is similar to how government politics ruins citizens' ability to rely on information being spit out of the spin machine. So get focused and get out of the corporate politics game, which is only meant for your competitors to destroy themselves.

Constructive criticism is necessary for all managers. Even still, employees will often be overly sensitive and in denial of any negative comments coming from employment reviews, or even casual discussions. There is rarely a reasonable cause for an employee lower in the organization to criticize his supervisor; instead, the two should discuss any issues proactively and constructively. In the end, however, the boss is always right. And if you don't believe this to be true, he may show you the door. (This is yet another good reason to be the boss.)

Firing someone is the hardest task you will have to undertake in business. If you can get past that professionally, everything else will be relatively easy.

The object is to hire much more often than you fire in order to continue building your winning team and allowing your business to grow. If you have to fire a lot of people, then you are probably making too many hiring mistakes.

OPTIMIZE HUMAN RESOURCES' COMMUNICATIONS

The main expenses in almost any business are payroll, employee benefits, and payroll taxes. So exclusively hiring the sort of people who, like you, will work harder and longer than the average employee will go a long way towards your ultimate success as a company.

When you are running a business, one of the most important tricks of the trade is effective communication among employees and management. You need to stay in touch with your staff and make sure the whole team is working diligently on your goals.

It's important to communicate your ideas and feelings freely and regularly with the relevant participants at departmental meetings to help boost morale and advance the organization. Think through what you want to accomplish and how it can best be done. Do not hold pent up frustrations simply because you feel a project moves too slowly or not as planned—just keep working on it.

All the tasks that you decide are required to meet your goals should be put on an up-to-date to-do list as they come up and then completed assiduously. This can help you distance your organization even further from competitors who overlook this same simple organizational opportunity.

Casual conversations "at the water cooler" can often generate good information flow. In a relaxed environment where people have their guard down, they tend to conduct "free association" and share their strategic enthusiasm with others who are in their business peer group. Aside from new ideas that are uncovered, chit chat serves as another Best Practices sounding board for existing initiatives.

Management should welcome input from employees on all matters, but once a decision is final, there is no need for harping about one not getting his way or hard feelings. Business is business. Nothing should be a personal attack or be perceived as one.

Trying to do ambitious projects on a budget, against fierce competition, can only be done with a rigorous commitment to goals, and without any negative feelings. If you have something to say to management or an individual regarding an area that you would like to help improve, you should say it directly and in private.

When a manager, who is responsible for a project, asks someone to complete a particular task, it is then that person's responsibility and must be on his or her to-do list until the task is complete. A supervisor should not have to delegate the same task more than once. If someone cannot handle the task because of time, skill, or other constraints, the supervisor should be made aware so they can then reassign the task as soon as possible.

In return, staff should not only react to management's demands but should push the envelope to a new level by offering to take on new responsibilities, which will advance the company and therefore themselves. All employees should be cross-trained in multiple responsibilities so they are as productive as possible. Everyone's responsibilities should be clear because the whole team needs to be on the same page for everyone to succeed.

FIRE THE DESERVING

Firing someone is the most difficult task in running a business. Not everyone is cut out for this because it can go against many people's natural instincts. However, as unpleasant as it may be, if you want to be a boss and ensure the best for your company, then it's a skill you must master.

There may be times when you need to fire friends or family members who are your partners or employees. Firing someone in general is difficult—firing someone close to you is even harder. But if they do not follow the letter of your written and verbal agreements, and they have been provided ample, direct warnings, then they have to go, or you, too, are being negligent.

If someone is dragging down your otherwise effective team, then it's like a hole in a dam. If your competitor applies the same amount of money as you do to an employee who is better than yours, then this will nip at your market position. Of course, you need to work with people who you trust. But can you also trust them to protect and enhance your market position?

Managers and employees should be judged on their results alone. Being a hard-working, nice, well-intentioned, and well-qualified person or friend to the boss should never negate the importance of the financial outcome of that person's presence in the company.

Cronyism and nepotism are not profitable. You can't let nice guys and gals who are your buddies or relatives negatively affect the otherwise positive flow of the organization, its morale, or its operational results. Even if their weaknesses can legitimately be construed as honest mistakes, it just doesn't matter. If they are not benefiting the company financially, they will ultimately have to go—the sooner the better.

From a self-preservation perspective and despite your affection for most of the characteristics of this individual who you ostensibly "like," the most important characteristic of a business always overrides anything else—profit. Profit for a company is equivalent to the oxygen mammals need in their evolutionary pursuit. If you are not acting in an evolutionary way by weeding out weak characteristics, you are not optimizing your business, and your competitors will eat away at your profit margin until you fail.

You don't need a traditional pyramid-shaped organizational chart for your company to succeed. Instead, you might be able to do much of your human resources scaling plan through independent contractors, or even friends, family, and former coworkers. You could even hire a delicate, cost-effective balance of telecommuters, employees, and contractors. Either way, the goal is to get scale and instill efficiency throughout your organization to give you a leveraged market position.

NATURE OF HUMAN RESOURCES

Human Resources Management (HRM or just HR), is basically a fancy term for "people". At the most fundamental stage, your HRM team should know their roles: deal with hiring, firing, training, and interpersonal issues.

Beyond the basics, your human resources specialists should offer a slew of qualifications because they are in charge of one of the most important components of your company—your team. Since his job is to fuse together the company's competitive needs with the greater demands of the employees, the person to fill the HRM role would be someone who has a loyalty to you and your SOPs, is trustworthy, and believes in building a team filled with real people who have real values, like yourself.

The HRM's objective, as stated by Schwind, Das & Wagar (2005), is this: "Human resource management aims to improve the productive contribution of individuals while simultaneously attempting to attain other societal and individual employee objectives." Wikipedia claims the objective of the HR role is "to maximize the return on investment from the organization's human capital."

Responsibilities of HRM include hiring, determining compensations, completing evaluations of performance, offering promotions, improving personal relations, and planning, and they should uphold these responsibilities effectively, fairly, legally, and consistently.

For your HR people to bring value to your company, the research done by The Conference Board found the following six "people-related activities":

1) Effectively managing and utilizing people;

2) Tying performance appraisal and compensations to competencies;

3) Developing competencies that enhance competitiveness;

4) Increasing the innovation, creativity, and flexibility necessary to enhance competitiveness;

5) Applying new approaches to work process design, succession planning, career development, and inter-organizational mobility; and

6) Managing the implementation and integration of technology through improved staffing, training, and communication with employees.

When going through the hiring process, be sure to outline your qualifications and specifications, so they are clear, honest, and fair. As a result, you should end up with more than just a fancy term for a person, but instead a high performing HR program.

Some managers see their HR role as "laying down the law" and "keeping people in line." However, that attitude is not conducive to the teamwork required within the organization. Typically, younger and less experienced managers are the ones who disregard this lesson. Building a team is a matter of trust and communication; talk to each other.

CHAPTER 7:
Get Off Your Tuchus and Go Sell

CONTACT MANAGEMENT

When you start a new business, maintaining your contacts is one of the first things you absolutely must do thoroughly, correctly, and perpetually—and it is probably one of the easiest and least expensive projects ahead of you relative to the value it will bring. Thankfully, the days of awkward and overpriced contact management software have come to an end.

It is surprising to see that a large portion of the business community takes no interest in proper contact management since technology has made it so easy to keep your information in systems such as SalesForce.com, SugarCRM, Act, or Goldmine.

Systems like these can store all of your contact names, addresses, phone and fax numbers, while integrating the data with your business calendar, phone services, PDA, Word documents, fax software, e-mail, web links, and web data.

As a side note, we are big critics of Outlook for several reasons, including that it is the most virus-prone software in existence, and it is controlled by Microsoft.

In your contact manager, you should import, key-in, save, and update detailed information on all possible leads or contacts including calendar items, dated notes, callback dates, their current service providers, their industries, quality rankings, size rankings, income rankings, links to press accounts and industry reports, and even their birthdays, partners' names, and kids' names.

With this consolidated data set, you can easily query the contact records when required, and pull up only the records that meet your select criteria, such as everyone who has a birthday this month, or every client organization with more than one million dollars of annual revenue, or every person with whom you went to college.

You must assertively build your data set year after year with all potentially relevant sales or commerce contacts, and ensure your follow-ups are well-timed and organized, so you can contact just the right people at just the right times to create the most long term cash flow.

If you have organized your contact management system properly, then having huge amounts of data will not be clutter; instead, it will be power at your fingertips.

The key is to have as much data as possible about each lead stored in the right fields, and to make sure every lead has a calendar date for when they are to be reviewed or contacted again. If you have determined they are a critical lead and a likely deal, then the calendar date is tomorrow. If you decide the lead is unlikely to ever close, then you can make it five years from now or delete it. In each case, your data set will be clean and meet a logical, simple business flow.

The most important source of data for you to gather and input is your personal network of contacts which includes the people you have met or solicited within your immediate business community. But this is a relatively low volume of contacts to work with compared to the broader community of those who you have yet to meet.

Vast additional raw data to upload and cull through are sold in electronic form and can be easily imported to your contact management system (generally comma-delimited ASCII text files are the easiest to move around).

One of your first tasks as a prospective business owner is to do your research, at the library as well as on the Internet, for the best sources of information in your chosen industry while taking in to account your target service area. Also, ask any of your colleagues or friends who might have insight into your industry and get referrals to additional data sources.

Decide what geographical area you want to market in (your target geographical market), and what types of customers you are trying to attract (your target consumer), and then make sure you have all the available data on every one of them.

From there, the data has to be heavily manipulated in order to allow you to extract the most pertinent information at just the right time. Again, a hard follow-up calendar date and complete data for each record are keys to your sales and marketing success, allowing you to efficiently generate good leads (lead-gen) and scale your volume.

The contact management system is not just for sales. It includes sections with employees and your personal friends if you want, along with sections for vendors and competitors, among any other data you choose to add.

For security purposes, these programs easily allow any group, individual record, or part of a record to become private by its creator.

For one source of data, you can get electronic versions of the "yellow pages" and similar directories covering your target geographic markets, and then upload records from select zip codes and industries that you want to work within.

You can then see what information is available on the Internet about each company, and you can purchase filtered lists, cleaned of extraneous data, to merge with all your original data. The web social network, LinkedIn, is a fantastic source for potential sales prospects and related information.

Often, Chambers of Commerce and government commerce agencies have extensive lists of business information available electronically. You need to get all of the data you can from all relevant sources and filter through the information repeatedly.

Ultimately, you will be able to personalize large volumes of e-mail, faxes, form mail, presentations, brochures, phone calls, all while efficiently scheduling, documenting, and sharing large amounts of data. You will be able to communicate a multitude of tailored messages better, faster, and easier than your competitors.

The bottom line is that if you don't optimize your contact management, you will be in the same marginal class as all the folks who are not at the top of their respective business categories. Assertive contact management cannot be overlooked since this process involves inexpensive leads that result in large profits.

One good example of the power of contact management relates to keeping track of your competitors. If you maintain a field in your contact manager program called "current service provider" (denoting the competitor of yours who your prospect is currently giving their money to), and you have been updating this field across thousands of sales prospects for years, you can target your competitors for extinction one at a time as they expose their own shortcomings.

You can instantly identify all of the potential customers in your database who work with any given competitor, as long as you have marked them over time in the ordinary course of business and in the correct field in your contact management system.

If you know of a particular weakness of a competitor at any set time, you can exploit it by instantly identifying and contacting his customers with a targeted sales promotion, which may allow you to take away those customers.

The most important—and time-consuming—part of contact management is cleaning out the raw data files. Right from the start, you should focus on filling in the field that lists the proper person who will be in the position to purchase your product, and that is within your predetermined market niche or geography, even if that's the whole world. So to the extent you lack this information, you or an associate need to call each of your target businesses, e-mail them, "Google" them, or go visit them in an attempt to uncover the data.

In addition, you should search each organization's website to collect further information. You should be able to copy and paste the most relevant information off the websites to the notes field in the contact manager. On the web, you can find articles that include information on your prospects, too. In Google, for example, you would enter +"Acme Corporation" +president +email to uncover the e-mail address and name of the president of your target prospect from a press release, a conference he attended, or even his own website or blog.

Alternatively, you can try to find the common syntax used at their company with other employees by discovering their domain and typing into Google "@acmecorporation.com", including the quote marks. This might find the record for Mary Jones to be mjones@acmecorporation.com, and Tom Williams to be twilliams@acmecorporation.com, so then if you know the president is John Smith you can assume he utilizes the same syntax in his e-mail and try to contact him at jsmith@acmecorporation.com. If that doesn't work, don't give up: try js@acmecorporation.com, john@acmecorporation.com, and so on. Or call the secretary and pretend you know something and are important, and ask for the president of the company or his e-mail address. In any event, persistence truly pays.

Bingo! You just bypassed a bunch of bureaucracy and got to the boss. Even though you may ultimately be ignored or rejected, statistically speaking, it's another "notch on your belt," and having it over with means you will be one step closer to the ones who won't ignore you.

As you continuously collect additional information on your prospects, you will find that you are able to understand them better. As a result, you will be capable of offering solutions that are ever more tailored to their specific needs, while relating to them in ways that you could not have predicted without that research.

Moreover, you can easily share leads, information, and notes with your own team and your business partners if you have a reliable CRM with trained users and tight security policies.

Most notably, you will realize that you have common associates from the business community who can potentially provide you with a pyramid of referrals, thereby hastening opening and closing deals.

Understanding the targets will help you focus your service offerings and sales approach to increase the percentage of deals you close. In turn, this will save you time and make you more money—yet again. Whatever you can do to reach an ever-expanding number of prospects will provide you with exponential financial benefit. Yes, I realize you appreciate all these moneymaking ideas. While I do not need gifts directly, you can help improve the world efficiently and thank me at the same time by donating to Grassroots.org.

Keep in mind that you can't waste time on prospects if there is a low likelihood of closing. You need to get as many relevant prospects as possible in your contact management system and sort through them by natural selection. That means you will be left with a bunch of unqualified records—a low percentage of the total but a large number nonetheless—which can be kept in the database and calendar with a callback or review date far in the future. These records should not represent any problems; instead, they will only represent potential opportunity as the best prospects can rise to the top of the calendar.

As you sift through and re-sort large numbers of prospects, you will be left with many unsuccessful attempts in order to get to the successful closes. The goal is to constantly expand your deal closing success rate while simultaneously increasing the daily number of new prospects being reviewed. The review itself should be as automated as possible and delegated to lower level co-workers when possible. This saves you precious deal-closing time for good quality prospects.

BUILD A WINNING SALES TEAM

You can teach someone selling techniques but not the natural ability it takes to sell, so always hire the most capable people. Like your other employees, your sales force should be, at minimum, well-organized, self-disciplined, and great communicators. Your sales team is your face to the outside world so make sure you hire the cream of the crop.

Preferably, each employee reports to one boss and one chief oversees the whole department. Selling is largely an independent activity. Don't delegate the same tasks or territories to multiple people. It is more important for each individual sales executive to develop a unique relationship with his or her client base.

When training your sales team, make sure they understand that people are buying the benefits of the product, not its features. For example, don't tell your sales prospects about the bells and whistles that are included with your "widget." Instead, tell your client how widgets can help save them millions, which would then help them go on vacation sooner.

Make sure your team knows how and when to ask rational, pertinent questions to prospects mixed in with the small talk, and make sure they LISTEN to the answers carefully. Not listening to what a customer says is a key failure for many salespeople and businesses in general. You may be able to tell from subtle intonations what the customer really takes to heart, and then if necessary, instantly adjust your sales "pitch" accordingly.

Usually, you should have a semi-formal presentation and then a casual question and answer period, often over lunch. But the most important aspects of your pitch are not in the details; it's in your positive attitude and clear, confident speech. Demonstrate mutual concern with your prospect and establish a human bond to increase your closing rate.

WIN WITH A RATIONAL SALES STRATEGY

When you are out in the field making sales, you are representing your product or service, your company, and possibly, your industry at large. It's crucial that you and your sales staff create a serious sales plan from day one to represent your products and services with a professional image.

You also need to make sure that all of your marketing material is consistent with your sales message. Furthermore, all of the material should go through a thorough review process by sending cycles of ideas and marketing text around to trusted, qualified marketing managers and other professionals, usually via e-mail attachments or on-line applications like BaseCamp.

From the first phone call to a prospective client, to the days and weeks after a contract has been signed, your salespeople represent you and your company to clients and the outside world, so make certain you spend the necessary resources to give them the best ongoing training and support.

When calling a new potential client, salespeople need to ask the gatekeeper (secretary, receptionist, assistant, spouse, vice president, and so forth) specifically who is in charge of their service area. Double check to make sure you will be connected to the best decision-maker. (Joining the networks LinkedIn and FaceBook gives you access to much of the info you might need and fills in pieces of a puzzle that can be further developed by doing basic research on your prospects in Google.)

Befriend the gatekeeper and ask as many questions as you can get away with because they can often open locked doors. (Examples of potential questions include: "How's the weather in Houston?"; "How do I spell her last name?"; "Can you tell me how to find your website?"; "Would you mind if I sent her a brief e-mail to outline our offer?"; "How long have you been in business?"; "How about those Redskins?", and so on.) As you see, the object is to establish a personal relationship that has the potential to grow over time, which might create the trust necessary for a broader, longer-term relationship with the prospect's company.

Every customer wants (and you must give them) personal service. Since you will have so much time and energy invested in providing the best services, your sales targets may as well be the big fish. You will be qualified to impress them, and they can afford your services and products.

One primary reason to target ostensibly high-level prospects is so you don't waste time giving fantastic service to people who are not in the position to make future serious commercial decisions and referrals. Those customers would only be of marginal benefit to your long-term goals, whereas, a wealthy VIP may be able to purchase your high margin services regularly, and introduce you to his equally valuable peers in an ever-compounding process.

Everything and everyone somehow ties together. Connect those dots. All positive human links can be of value. The people with the strongest business and social connections, and the most impressive past successes, are the most beneficial to associate with your own expanding corporate-social-charitable network. You want to know all of their friends and business associates so you can speak more intelligibly about their line of business and create more sustainable relationships.

Always make the links obvious so they can be strengthened and expanded to your advantage. Do the proper industry research, not just about the product or service that you are selling, but also about the people in that industry and your particular sales prospects.

Have you heard of the game "Six Degrees of Kevin Bacon"? It helps prove how a human referral system can connect you to almost anyone you want to reach, as long as you flesh out the network effectively. Go for the big names, and make sure you are always developing new references to get there.

Be quick and efficient once you are speaking with the right person so you can make more calls, set up more meetings, and submit more proposals (and so they don't quickly tire of you).

Be assertive but not too pushy. Be very polite—say "yes, ma'am/sir," "yes, please," "thanks," and "I appreciate your help."

Contact multiple people at the same company, if that's what's necessary to close the deal. Nevertheless, don't appear as though you are trying to go behind the back of your primary contact. There isn't always a clear chain of command for service provision, and nobody will be offended if you politely push a good deal through the bureaucracy. Always have a positive or neutral tone of voice, even in negative, frustrating situations.

Once you have an appointment, go about your first meeting the right way. Always ask your sales prospect his time frame and budget. If he doesn't know this, then he is not close to buying what you are selling.

Be confident with the fact that you are the best in each service area so you are being honest when you tell your prospects so. They will likely notice your confidence and will have confidence in you in return. In fact, if you don't intend on trying to be the best, then get a new job.

Ask many open-ended questions to prospects, thereby eliciting their critical involvement in the sales process. Memorize questions and answers; learn who to ask, which questions to ask, and when to ask them. Clients love to talk about themselves and it is an invitation into their world. Moreover, you need to document all the information you can get since it adds future strategic value to your marketing arsenal.

Be fearless; if you are hesitant or nervous to ask the right questions and make a pitch, you aren't going to sell anything. You have nothing to lose unless somehow you are establishing a bad reputation by being annoying.

Keep tools handy like industry and marketing directories, databases, industry pricing and inventories, emerging ideas and questions, references, and URLs (in your bookmarks management application). Know the answers to questions that customers might ask, by memory if possible.

In your closing process, precisely know which stage you are in and what action any items or objections need in order to be managed properly. Once those items are effectively dealt with, you should have a completed deal unless other objections exist. If that's the case, then deal with those issues immediately. For the most part, objections are repetitive, so you should know how to counter each one in advance.

Send marketing items to your prospects and customers consistently over the life of your relationship with the purpose of keeping your company name in your contact's mind: i.e., printed brochures, concise PowerPoint presentations, specials, faxes, newsletters, business cards, calendars, and other ad specialties (like pens, shirts, magnets, mouse pads, bumper stickers, relevant press clippings, and so on). Don't forget to work with them on-line, too, by e-mailing relevant links, press releases, and other information.

According to Jay Conrad Levinson, the author of business bestseller Guerilla Marketing, an average prospect needs to be exposed to your message nine times before he is amenable to become a customer. Since the prospect only sees or hears your message one out of three times when you attempt to reach them, that would mean it takes twenty-seven attempted exposures to begin to saturate each prospect effectively with your brand or messaging.

The greater quantity and variety of exposures, the better—referrals, press articles, fax, mail, newspaper ads, radio, affinity groups, friends, and on-line articles are all helpful in getting your message out.

As always, spelling and grammar in marketing material is critical—don't get any of it wrong. Optimize your overall verbiage and word flow so your message can be fully absorbed by the highest proportion of prospects. Work with creative marketing people to help you out.

Copious notes on each sales call and meeting should be kept in your contact manager so you can gauge the effectiveness of your sales process, and use that information to tailor your future messages.

Call clients back in a reasonable amount of time after meetings, or send letters and faxes so they don't forget you. Ask for good days and times to do follow-ups if they are generally hard to contact, and ask gatekeepers for the same information.

You must follow-up thoroughly on leads or else all the time and money used on your background and introductory work is wasted, and all leverage is lost! But reprioritize follow-ups according to your perception of the prospect's likelihood of bearing fruit. In this case, your contact manager (the best are SalesForce.com and SugarCRM) once again proves to be critical, particularly its calendar functions.

Do a lot of hand holding for demanding prospects. On average, this will be worth the cost and effort for you and will lead to future strong sales and referrals. If you can please the most demanding customers, then you can please the not-so-demanding ones even more.

Establish long-term personal relationships with targets and clients to the extent that it aligns with your goals. Make it easy instead of overwhelming or overly complex for clients to buy what you are offering. Then make sure to literally ask for the sale by saying, "What do you think?" "Are you ready?" and "Can I bring you the contract?" Then sit quietly and let them answer. Above all, listen to any objections you will have to overcome.

If the answer is "no," you will have to accept the rejection and move on until your sales process suggests it's time to call on that prospect later, if ever. Don't be discouraged if your offer fails. But when a customer is ready to sign up, do not give him the opportunity to change his mind—make the arrangements by phone, fax, and e-mail ASAP or, better yet, set up meetings with the contract in hand.

Statistical modeling will help you organize and analyze the tests of your business activities. This can be especially effective in Internet commerce where you can electronically measure the effects of new navigation, graphics, text, partner programs, contextual advertising strategies, and so on, while dynamically improving your results on a real time basis. Profits generated from your successful advertising tests can fund additional, more permanent advertising investments. This is the ideal.

When you make proposals to sell your services, they should often be based on standard company templates that are then customized to meet each specific proposal at hand. They also must reflect the accurate budgets involved as well as the reasonable time frames for benchmark activities. Proposals must be good-looking and accurate, spell-checked, and grammatically correct.

Make an estimate of what the customers can spend since often what a client wants may not be what he can afford. And detail his specific needs so he knows the proposal is tailored for him.

Hit lots of leads simultaneously since only a minority of deals will ultimately close no matter how promising they appear throughout the process.

Know precisely which services you wish to sell to each prospect based on his likely requirements. Suggest solutions based on previous customers in similar situations.

See what others in the prospect's industry do for their solutions.

Know who your existing clients are and how to use them as references.

Consider doing a tag team on deals, exposing the prospect to several trustworthy, friendly, capable co-workers. This is often very successful

When possible, use your prospects' consultants to help close the deals. Likewise, consultants might give you access to additional business from their other customers if they appreciate your service. Consultants are therefore leveraged prospects who should be considered high priority.

Once you've made a sale, check up on your customers and try to sell them additional services while also attempting to get references; highlight your product line expansions and diversifications.

Plant lots of seeds that could grow into good deals and opportunities far in the future. Build a pyramid of referrals that will spin off business indefinitely.

Recommend add-on services. Say, "I will be in your building at two o'clock. May I stop in for ten minutes to show you/tell you about…?" This way, you'll spread a wide net over various markets while still getting the most out of each individual contact.

Consider offering your prospects a questionnaire, if that makes sense for your product, and then take their feedback seriously to help improve future offerings.

Document the good ideas and solutions that you learn in the field and include them in your Best Practices or Standard Operational Procedures master documents, so they are easily at hand when you want to reuse them and teach them to others.

It's possible, despite your best efforts and investments in advertising trials, that you have been unable to prove the effectiveness of traditional advertising for your business. Advertising is a technique that should be abandoned in favor of other investments if not directly proven profitable. Marketing is a broader process that includes how you and your product are presented so it cannot be removed from your long-term business plan. You should have a sound advertising strategy that might include not advertising at all.

Since the advent of Google's AdWords/AdSense platform and Yahoo's Overture platform, both leveraging the very profitable market they have created for dynamic contextual advertising links, along with older school applications like Advertising.com (now part of AOL) and DoubleClick (now part of Google), traditional advertising has taken new, innovative forms. Now, businesses, even with small budgets, can more effectively reach their target markets and contend against larger competitors through Internet advertising, which is currently best done with text link advertising via on-line bidding processes.

Google has been the primary force in the democratization of advertising. Suddenly taking brands global isn't just for big corporations with large scale marketing budgets and strategies. Also, keep your eye on companies like SpotRunner, ReachLocal, SEO.com, and their competitors, which meld the better aspects of the Google targeting and bidding platforms with more traditional, local, and Internet advertising. Don't be surprised if Google or its wannabe competitors spend enormous dollars one day to attempt to gain control over this niche of the search advertising marketplace.

With democratized campaigns, your ads can be more controlled allowing you to precisely test and measure your marketing strategies. Aspiring ad networks beyond Google and Yahoo are getting in the mix. With friends like these, traditional advertising might no longer be the best way to reach your marketing objectives. Most likely, each year you will be able to justify spending a greater portion of your marketing dollars on non-traditional Internet-centric media at the expense of traditional broadcast and print channels.

For instance, with your own small advertising budget, you can effectively expose your company using Google AdWords (adwords.google.com). You only pay when your ad is clicked on (Pay per Click/PPC), and you have granular control of your campaign to adjust details like budgets, keywords, and dates, whenever you choose. You can make as many changes to the advertisements as you want until you get the desired results without breaking your budget.

Google and Yahoo sell text link ads in a bidding process and have exact statistical "conversion" data with a multitude of ways to adjust and precisely measure your customer acquisitions. This is often an excellent option for companies to test. SEO.com, Yield Software, ReachLocal, and their competitors can help manage this same on-line advertising phenomena cost-effectively, and potentially very profitably, for companies without adequate internal resources.

CONCLUSION

Every business has a chance to succeed. Yet only 50% make it through their first year, and only 10% see beyond their fifth anniversary. These businesses cite hundreds of reasons why they've failed. In most cases, however, the simple truth is that management made fundamental mistakes.

To reduce the risk of wasting time and money, make sure you have sound business plans and a willingness to put in years of hard work. Invest in the best people, including a team of professionals, to help guide you. Adopt the Best Practices of industry leaders and improve on them daily. Be innovative and have customer-centric values. Stay focused at all times. Learn from the blips in your progress; don't let them derail you. Take two leaps forward for every one step back. Make more sales calls and close a higher percentage of them every day.

Finally, when your business is successful and you have made your millions, take the time to give back to your community and the world by engaging in the charitable causes that mean the most to you.

We hope that some of the ideas presented in this document will help you build the business of your dreams and that you will become a catalyst for positive social change. Go for it!

PART 2 - THE PROCESS OF ENTREPRENEURSHIP LESSONS

The focus of this second part is to help you develop an understanding of how business ideas are generated. At the end of this second part you should be able to identify different methods of generating business ideas and opportunity identification; examine business concepts; identify different resources essential for business success; and how to implement and manage a business venture.

After you finish reading you should:

1. Understand the entrepreneurial process;

2. Appreciate the key stages in the process;

3. Understand the process through which business ideas are evaluated.

Lesson 1 - Generating Business Ideas

In this lesson you should be able to:

1. Identify the steps in the entrepreneurial process;

2. Discuss some of the methods of generating ideas;

Introduction

Scanning the business environment means that the prospective entrepreneur needs to do some research. If research proves the business idea to be a viable business opportunity you can start drawing up your business. Let's examine how business ideas are generated.83

How to Identify Business Opportunities

A business opportunity starts with a business idea. A prospective entrepreneur must look for a creative idea that can be transformed into a business opportunity by scanning the business environment. Working through the next part will help you to understand how to identify business opportunities and generate business ideas much better.

How to Generate Business Ideas

Scanning the business environment will help the entrepreneur to identify business ideas.

A business idea is the starting point of the journey to setting up a business. Business ideas are based on given situations and will differ from place to place and also from entrepreneur to entrepreneur.85

We can, therefore, see business ideas as:

❖ Dreams about creative ways of meeting the community's needs/wants

❖ Dreams of creative solutions to the communities' problems

❖ Innovative ways of improving on what is already being done, and

❖ A creative means of meeting the fantasies and dreams of community members for luxury and a better life.

Business ideas may come from problems or situations, needs and wants, our interests and hobbies, as well as the natural resources around us. Coming up with a good business idea or even just changing old ideas into new ones, however, requires some creativity from the prospective entrepreneur.

What is Creative Thinking and how can it be enhanced?

Creativity is a way of thinking, coming up with new and innovative ways of solving problems. It is the mental attitude of always trying to improve on existing products and services. Remember that we said earlier that creativity is something that can be developed. Look at the following insert to see how you can become creative.

Remember that generating ideas or identifying opportunities can be improved by using creativity methods.

Creativity Methods

Explanation

Brainstorming

Decide what the problem is and give ideas on ways to solve it. Just let the ideas flow and write down all of it. Do not comment on whether they are good or bad.

Attribute analysis

Make a list of a few existing products and services and create a list of attributes (characteristics) for each of them. By combining various attributes, you may be able to come up with an entirely new product or service.

Problem redefinition

Define a problem that you or others experience and write it down. Think of ways in which the problem could be solved by introducing a new product or service.

Manipulation

Make a list of some new products and services and think of ways in which you can change them, e.g., make it smaller, and change the colour, shape or package.

Forced connections

Take two ideas or products that have little or nothing in common and try to make a connection between the two, e.g., bed + food = bed and breakfast.

Mind mapping

Mind mapping is a way to help you think creatively and gives you a picture of groups of ideas that you can examine without losing your main idea.

For example: Choose a word or group of words and write them down in the center of a page. Think of anything that has some link with the word. Write it down and draw a line connecting it to the central word(s).

Good viable business ideas:

➤ Focus on the needs and wants of consumers;

➤ Must be able to provide consumers with the necessary goods and services, and

➤ Improve on the existing product and make it ➤ more attractive for consumers

Turning Ideas into Business Opportunities

By now, you should have at least one idea for a new business venture. Maybe, you are wondering when an idea becomes an opportunity. Considering the wants and needs of people in your community is only the first step towards identifying a business opportunity. There are many other issues that you need to take into account as well. Remember that we said earlier in the unit that good ideas are not necessarily good opportunities. Opportunities are ideas that work, and that can be turned into successful businesses.

There are many potentially profitable business opportunities in the business environment, and any individual can enter into business. What about you? Do you also possess the quality of being creative and turning a business idea into an opportunity?

The followings are indicators/characteristics of a good business opportunity:

★ There should be an actual market or a demand for the product and/or service.

★ The business should have the capacity to generate profits.

★ The business should be able to get the factor inputs it requires for operation.

★ The business should be acceptable in the community.

Potential entrepreneurs should, therefore, look at factors that will have an impact on the business, such as government regulations, how much tax they need to pay, the current interest rates, social and cultural trends which might influence consumer demand, new innovations, available infrastructure, potential competitors, available resources needed, potential suppliers and potential customers. When all these factors prove to be positive and in favor of the entrepreneur, it means that his or her business idea can be a viable business opportunity. Keep in mind that changes in the business environment can present good business opportunities. As soon as the idea has been assessed and you have come up with the most promising business opportunities, you must proceed to evaluate them and identify the one that meets your business expectations and abilities.

When you have identified a potentially successful opportunity, you should assess whether it is indeed an attractive opportunity. Turning an opportunity into a successful business makes specific demands on the entrepreneur. You will now be introduced to sources of information that could be of value to you in evaluating your opportunity.

A lot of work goes into starting a business: you need to draw up a business plan, find investors, get loans, and look for employees. Before all that, however, you have to come up with your idea for a business. This could be a new product, service, or, method, but it has to be something that customers will pay money for.

The process of finding that very good business idea takes thought, creativity, and research, and sometimes it may come from a chaotic situation. If you are looking to be an entrepreneur, keep the following in mind when trying to come up with your business idea. The entrepreneur can use several methods to help generate and test new ideas, including focus groups, brainstorming, and problem inventory analysis.

METHODS OF GENERATING NEW IDEAS

Even with the wide variety of sources available, coming up with an idea to serve as the basis for the new venture can still be a difficult problem. The entrepreneur can use several methods to help generate and test new ideas, including focus groups, brainstorming, and problem inventory analysis.

Focus groups

Group of individuals providing information in a structured format is called a focus group. The group of 8 to 14 participants is simulated by comments from other team members in creatively conceptualizing and developing new product ideas to fulfill a market need.

Brainstorming

A group method of obtaining new ideas and solutions is called brainstorming. The brainstorming method for generating new ideas is based on the fact that people can be stimulated to greater creativity by meeting with others and participating in organized group experiences. Although most of the ideas generated from the group have no basis for further development, often a good idea emerges.

Problem inventory analysis

Problem inventory analysis uses individuals in a manner that is analogous to focus groups on generating new product ideas. However, instead of generating new ideas themselves, consumers are provided with a list of problems in a general product category. They are then asked to identify and discuss products in this category that have a particular problem. This method is often effective since it is easier to relate known products to suggest problems and arrive at a new product idea than to generate an entirely new idea by itself.

CREATIVE PROBLEM-SOLVING

Creative problem solving is a method for obtaining new ideas focusing on the parameters.

Brainstorming

The first technique, brainstorming, is probably the most well-known and widely used for both creative problems solving and idea generation. It is an unstructured process for generating all possible ideas about a problem within a limited time frame through the spontaneous contribution of the participants. All ideas, no matter how illogical, must be recorded, with participants prohibited from criticizing or evaluating during the brainstorming session.

Reverse brainstorming

Similar to brainstorming, but criticism is allowed and encouraged as a way to bring out possible problems with the ideas.

Synectics

Synectics is a creative process that forces individuals to solve problems through one of four analogy mechanisms: personal, direct, symbolic and fantasy. This forces participants to apply preconscious mechanisms consciously through the use of analogies to solve problems.

Gordon method

Gordon method is a method of developing new ideas when the individuals are unaware of the problem. With this approach, the entrepreneur starts by mentioning a general concept associated with the problem. The group responds by expressing some ideas.

Checklist method

Developing a new idea through a list of related issues is a checklist method of problem-solving.

Exercise by listening to how young entrepreneurs use their ideas to generate millions in viable business ventures especially in business network meeting to evaluate our approach.

Review and then reflect on your own business ideas. Evaluate if any of these approaches can assist in developing your business ideas to a profitable business venture.

There are many approaches used to generate business ideas. The Delphi Methodology is one of these methods. Here are six steps in the Delphi technique that could further analyze your business idea.

Watch the videos indicated in references and reflect on any five (5) of the decisions that proved to be mistaken.

https://www.youtube.com/watch?v=Wky9cLHTc7g&feature=youtu.be (CC-BY)

http://www.slideshare.net/Launchyourgenius/15-ideas-on-how-to-generate-new-ideas (CC BY SA)

http://www.preservearticles.com/201205183237/6-sequential-steps-in-delphi-technique.html

https://www.youtube.com/watch?

v=M7SqQnKuZOQ&feature=youtu.be (CC BY)

State whether the statement is True/False.

1. At the core of any business venture is an idea.

2. A determination to keep things the same taps into entrepreneurs' creativity.

3. Education, friends, hobbies can all be sources of start-up ideas for a business

4. The capacity to generate a loss or the lack of an actual market is a good indicator of a business opportunity that should not be perused.

5. Viable business ideas focus on the developer of the product.

6. A creative mindset is the death of new product development.

Summary

Generating a business idea is one of the first steps in the Entrepreneurial Process. In this process entrepreneurs screen all prospective ideas to evaluate their viability. Once a viable idea is to determine it is important to assess the business opportunities that can derive from that idea before investing resources in the business venture. In the next lesson, we will explore the elements that determine and influence the viability of a business opportunity.

Lesson 2 - Opportunity Identification

After taking this lesson you should be able to:

1. Identify sources of entrepreneurial opportunities
2. Distinguish between idea and opportunity
3. Evaluate an opportunity of giving information

Introduction

A business opportunity consists of four elements, all of which are to be present within the same time frame (window of opportunity) and most often within the same domain or geographical location before it can be claimed as a business opportunity. These four elements are:

- A need
- The means to fulfill the need
- A method to apply the means to fulfill the need and;
- A method to benefit

With any one of the elements missing, a business opportunity may be developed, by finding the missing element. A desirable characteristic is the combination of items to be unique. The more control an institution (or individual) has over the elements, the better they are positioned to exploit the opportunity and become a niche market leader99.

Entrepreneurship can be viewed as

· Recognizing change,

· Pursuing opportunity,

· Taking on risk and responsibility,

· Innovating,

· Making better (higher value) use of resources,

· Creating new value that is meaningful to customers,

· Doing it all over again and again.

Moreover, entrepreneurship is an attitude and the drive to pursue opportunity and create something new and of value.

Entrepreneurial Opportunities

Many different conditions in society can create entrepreneurial opportunities for new goods and services. Opportunity conditions arise from a variety of sources. At a broad societal level, they are present as the result of forces—such as changes in knowledge and understanding, the development of new technology, shifting demographics, political change, or changing attitudes and norms—that give rise to new preferences and concerns. These forces constantly open up new opportunities for entrepreneurs.

In relation to sustainability concerns, certain demographic shifts and pollution challenges create opportunities. For example, with 50 percent of the world's population, for the first time in history, now living in urban areas, city air quality improvement present opportunities for entrepreneurs.

The entrepreneur must first recognize the opportunity and then innovate by proposing a business solution that provides an attractive alternative to customers. A solution is just the first step in the process; the entrepreneur must also investigate the economic value of and business proposition emanating from that opportunity. They must research the market to understand how their potential product or service provides value to a customer and whether the amount a customer is willing to pay, which reflects the value of the product or service to the customer, exceeds the costs to provide that value, product, or service to the customer. In this way, the entrepreneur is contributing to economic growth and society by providing customers with goods and services whose costs to provide are less than their value to consumers.

An entrepreneur can come up with a new approach that meets a customer's need or want, but if not enough customers are willing or able to pay a price above the cost of that product or service, it will not be financially viable. Therefore, the opportunity becomes a true business opportunity when it is of sufficient scale and value—that is, revenues will cover costs and promise to offer net revenue above operating costs after the initial start-up investment expenditures are repaid.

Emerging markets

The definition of an emerging market is complex and inconsistent. The application and interpretation of this information vary depending on who is doing the analysis—a private sector business, the World Bank, the International Monetary Fund (IMF), the World Trade Organization (WTO), the United Nations (UN), or any number of global economic, political, and trade organizations. The different statistics, in turn, produce a changing number of countries that "qualify" as emerging markets. For many business people, the definition of an emerging market has been simply a country that was once a developing country but has achieved rapid economic growth, modernization, and industrialization.

During the last 20 years, the global business world has gone through drastic, but mostly positive changes. In the 1980s, international business was essentially an exclusive club of the 20 richest countries. This changed as dictatorships and command economies collapsed throughout the world. Countries that once prohibited foreign investment from operating on their soil and were isolated from international cooperation are now part of the global marketplace.

Knowing that there are wide inconsistencies, how do we define emerging markets consistently from the perspective of global businesses? First, understand that there are some common characteristics in terms of local population size, growth opportunities with changes in the local commercial infrastructure, regulatory and trade policies, efficiency improvements, and an overall investment in the education and well-being of the local population, which in turn is expected to increase local incomes and purchasing capabilities.

There are several major characteristics of emerging markets, which create "a comfortable and attractive environment for global business, foreign investment, and international trade. An emerging market country can be defined as a society transitioning from a dictatorship to a free- market-oriented economy, with increasing economic freedom, gradual integration within the global marketplace, an expanding middle class, improving standards of living and social stability and tolerance, as well as an increase in cooperation with multilateral institutions.

The category of emerging markets is complex, evolving, and subject to wide interpretation. So how then do savvy global professionals sort through all of this information? Managers focus on the criteria for emerging markets to take advantage of newly emerging ones. While there are differing opinions on which countries are emerging, it is clear that global businesses focus on the groups of countries offering strong domestic markets. Many of these emerging-market countries are also home to companies that are taking advantage of the improved business conditions there. These companies are becoming world-class global competitors in their industries. Regardless of which definition or classification is used, the largest emerging markets remain lucrative and promising.

Emerging markets, such as Brazil, Russia, India, and China (also collectively known as the BRIC countries), don't have the same needs or capabilities as those found in developed economies. For instance, disposable income levels are relatively low, the availability of basic utilities like water or electricity can be varied, and transportation and transportation infrastructure can be non-existent. While these emerging economies are attractive by virtue of their massive size, their different needs and capabilities pose unique challenges that are often overcome only through corporate innovation.

New Technologies

Technology, being a form of social relationship, always evolves. No technology remains fixed. Technology starts, develops, persists, mutates, stagnates, and declines, just like living organisms. The evolutionary life cycle occurs in the use and development of any technology. The technological changes that damage established companies are usually not radically new or difficult from a technological point of view. They do, however, have two important characteristics: First, they typically present a different package of performance attributes—ones that, at least at the outset, are not valued by existing customers. Second, the performance attributes that existing customers do value, improve at such a rapid rate that the new technology can later invade those established markets.

The process of how disruptive technology, through its requisite support net, dramatically transforms a certain industry. When the technology that has the potential for revolutionizing an industry emerges, established companies typically see it as unattractive: it is not something their mainstream customers want, and its projected profit margins are not sufficient to cover big-company cost structure. As a result, the new technology tends to get ignored for what's currently popular with the best customers. However, then another company steps in to bring innovation to a new market. Once the disruptive technology becomes established there, smaller-scale innovation rapidly raises the technology's performance on the attributes that mainstream customers' value.

Technology entrepreneurship lies at the heart of many important debates, including those around launching and growing firms, regional economic development, selecting the appropriate stakeholders to take ideas to market, and educating managers, engineers, and scientists. Technology entrepreneurship is an investment in a project that assembles and deploys specialized individuals and heterogeneous assets to create and capture value for the firm. What distinguishes technology entrepreneurship from other entrepreneurship types (e.g., Social entrepreneurship, small business management, and self-employment) is the collaborative experimentation and production of new products, assets, and their attributes, which are intricately related to advances in scientific and technological knowledge and the firm's asset ownership rights.

The Internet and social networking websites have been pivotal resources for the success and collaboration of many social entrepreneurs. In the twenty-first century, the Internet has become especially useful in disseminating information in short amounts of time. In addition to this, the Internet allows for the pooling of design resources using open source principles. These media allow ideas to be heard by broader audiences, help networks, and investors to develop globally and to achieve their goals with little or no start-up capital. For example, the rise of open-source appropriate technology as a sustainable development paradigm enables people all over the world to collaborate on solving local problems just as open-source software development leverages collaboration.

Social Changes

Social innovations are new strategies, concepts, ideas and organizations that meet the social needs of different elements which can be from working conditions and education to community development and health — they extend and strengthen civil society. Social innovation includes the social processes of innovation, such as open-source methods and techniques and also the innovations which have a social purpose— like online volunteering, microcredit, or distance learning.

Opportunity Evaluation

In the business world, good ideas must pass one test: can they generate a profit? No idea is good, ultimately, if it cannot pass this test. This means that someone somewhere has to pay you more money for your product or service than it costs to produce it. Is it that simple and that challenging? Perhaps the most important part of any business plan is an articulation of the customer. Why will they buy it, When, Where, and for how much?

Of course, other characteristics are important too: does the idea have a social good or at least do no harm? How challenging is it to make? Is it within the capabilities of the team? Sometimes student teams have great ideas but no way in the world by executing them. You may want to save your great idea until you've had a little more experience with something that's more manageable. Can you raise enough money to finance your idea? Often great ideas fail this test: simply put, they require too much capital to prove themselves.

Summary

In this Lesson, you examined how the changing demographics, emerging markets, new technologies, regulatory and social changes influence the viability of business opportunity in the market. Along with how to market and economic issues, competitive advantage and management issue plays a role in the evaluation of business opportunities.

Again, spend some time reflecting on your business venture. Are there any regulatory changes in your business environment that will impact your enterprise? How has the changing demographics in your culture impacted your business? How viable is your business opportunity?

Lesson 3 - Business Concepts

After taking this lesson you should be able to:

1. Define a business concept.

2. Identify at least four sources of business concepts.

3. Evaluate the steps in developing a business concept from an idea

Introduction

The first stage in seeking to establish a business is to conceptualize a business idea. It requires identification of a venture that can satisfy human wants and needs while generating a profit. In this section, you will define the business concept, identify various sources from which a business concept can emerge and outline the steps involved in developing a concept from an idea.

What is the business concept?

A business idea is a concept that can be used for financial gain that is usually centered on a product or service that can be offered for money. An idea is the first milestone in the process of building a successful business.

The characteristics of a promising business idea are:

- Innovative
- Unique
- Problem-solving
- Profitable

Sources of the business concept

1. Hobbies/Interests: A hobby is a favorite leisure-time activity or occupation. Many people, in pursuit of their hobbies or interests, have founded businesses. If, for example, you enjoy playing with computers, cooking, music, traveling, sport or performing, to name but a few, you may be able to develop it into a business.

2. Personal skills and experience: Over half of the ideas for successful businesses come from experiences in the workplace, e.g. a mechanic with experience in working for a large garage who eventually sets up his/her own car repair or a used car business. Thus, the background of potential entrepreneurs plays a crucial role in the decision to go into business as well as the type of venture to be created. Your skills and experience are probably your most valuable resource, not only in generating ideas but also in capitalizing on them.

3. Mass media: The mass media is a great source of information, ideas and often opportunity. Newspapers, magazines, television, and nowadays the Internet are all examples of mass media.

Take a careful look, for instance, at the commercial advertisements in the newspaper or magazine and you may well find businesses for sale. Well, one way to become an entrepreneur is to respond to such an offer. Articles in the printed press or on the Internet or documentaries on television may report on changes in fashions or consumer needs. For example, you may read or hear that people are now increasingly interested in healthy eating or physical fitness. You may also find advertisements calling for the provision of certain services based on skills. For example, accounting, catering or security. Alternatively, you may discover a new concept in which investors are required, such as a franchise.

4. Exhibitions: Another way to find the ideas for a business is to attend exhibitions and trade fairs. These are usually advertised on the radio or in newspapers; by visiting such events regularly, you will not only discover new products and services, but you will also meet sales representatives, manufacturers, wholesalers, distributors, and franchisers. These are often excellent sources of business ideas, information, and help in getting started.

5. Surveys: The focal point for a new business idea should be the customer. The needs and wants of the customer, which provide the rationale for a product or service, can be ascertained through a survey. Such a survey might be conducted informally or formally by talking to people – usually using a questionnaire or through interviews – and/or through observation. You may start by talking to your family and friends to find out what they think is needed or wanted that is not available. Alternatively, for example, whether they are dissatisfied with an existing product or service and what improvements or changes they would like to see. You can then move on and talk to people who are part of the distribution chain that is manufacturers, wholesalers, distributors, agents, and retailers. It would be useful to prepare beforehand a set of questions which might be put in a questionnaire or used in an interview. Given their close contact with customers, channel members have a good sense of what is required and what will not sell. Finally, you should talk to as many customers as possible – both existing and potential customers. The more information you can get from them, the better. Besides talking to people, you could also get information

through observation. For example, in deciding whether to open a shop on a particular street, you can observe and count the number of people going past on given days and besides talking to people, you can also get information through observation.

6. Complaints: Complaints and frustrations on the part of customers have led to many a new product or service. Whenever consumers complain bitterly about a product or service, or when they hear someone says 'I wish there were..." or "If only there were a product/service that could... ", you have the potential for a business idea. The idea could be to set up a rival firm offering a better product or service, or it might be a new product or service which could be sold to the firm in question and/or others.

Think about your business concept. Answer the following questions in paragraph form.

1. Where did you get that business idea?

2. How long did it take that idea to incubate?

3. What type of feedback did you receive from persons you shared that business idea with? How did their feedback affect you?

4. How can your idea be turned into something meaningful?

The feasibility study

Conducting a feasibility study for a proposed business concept (incubator) can achieve a number of important objectives and, if properly done, can provide a solid basis for judging the economic and political viability of the proposed project. The feasibility study represents the first in a series of early development phases that, for planning purposes, can be described as follows:

• Feasibility: 3 months

• Development: 9 months

• Renovation: 3-12 months

• Early-stage operations (up to anticipated break-even point): 18 months.

A feasibility study should also reveal examples of critical errors made on other incubator programs. Such errors might involve facility and site selection, the structure of the governing board, funding arrangements, income assumptions, or the nature of the business assistance program. An adequate feasibility study will answer essential questions about how to proceed in a systematic fashion and how to secure funding during all the phases of incubator development. Indeed, a thorough study by a qualified consultant can and should provide the information necessary to determine whether the project should be pursued.

Building support

A core group committed to starting a business incubator must recognize that its efforts cannot be pursued in a vacuum. The dream of a few must become the dream of many. An incubator represents a significant community investment, both practically and symbolically, and requires broad-based community support to be feasible. Engaging in this process should clarify the prospects for starting an incubator. The process should help to identify potential sites, funding sources, project champion from key organizations, and sources of assistance and support, both individual and organizational. The process may, however, also uncover serious impediments to realizing the project.

Identifying and securing stakeholders

A stakeholder is any group or individual who can affect or is affected by the achievement of an organization's objectives. While each incubator's circumstance is unique, anticipated stakeholders would likely include local and state governments and a variety of public and private sector organizations (universities, major corporations) interested in fostering new business development in the region. Stakeholders might also include economic development organizations that could fund the rehabilitation of a facility and/or the operation of the incubator program. The support of these stakeholders is critical to initiating an incubator program. At the same time, potential supporters of the incubator effort understandably have varied motivations and expectations. Their level of understanding of the purposes and methods of business incubation will vary widely.

Stakeholders need to be identified and then cultivated. The first step is to secure a commitment from potential stakeholders who have the strongest interest and who are most likely to provide financial support for the endeavor. Once stakeholders have committed to the project, the organizational structure needs to be formalized. A governing body, typically a board of directors, provides the organizational vehicle for maintaining, building, and strengthening the commitment to the incubator program.

Identifying a market niche

A business incubator will operate in a particular locale with its own rich history, so it must act with an eye to the regional economy and institutions. Therefore, to become an accepted part of this complex social fabric, an incubator must establish its distinctiveness and unique purpose. From a business perspective, the incubator needs to identify its market niche. Successful businesses carefully attend to the work of defining the market position of their products and services about their competitors, as well as to modifying their market position in response to changing customer preferences.

Developing a market niche for a business incubator requires similar attention to these tasks. An incubator's competitor comes from the spheres of real estate and economic development. Within the real estate market, the incubator must distinguish itself from other multiple-tenant properties. For a technology-related incubator, the distinction may be readily apparent, for example, in that incubator facilities may offer wet and dry lab space. Incubators also differ from conventional real estate agents in that they often offer short-term leases and flex-space for a company's expansion. Certainly, rent subsidization can be attractive to cash-poor start-ups. The availability of shared support services is another appealing feature of incubator facilities, although the provision of such services by for-profit organizations has become a growth industry.

The Formation Process

The basic structure of an incubator facility is determined by owner attributes and regional demographics. The following owner/sponsor classifications can generally be applied:

· Private

· Local government

· University

- State government
- Private nonprofits
- Federal government

A typical organizational format includes executive and advisory boards, a CEO or operations manager, and support staff. Selections for board positions and other representative forums may come from the following: private enterprise, educational institutions, government, organized labour, development and investment community, and private citizens.

Strategic Planning

Strategic planning compels incubator management to confront tough issues. How will the incubator continue to operate if revenue projections from rental income are not achieved? How will major facility repairs (for example, a ruptured boiler) be paid for? Addressing these worst-case scenarios through strategic planning can provide both a clear course of action if things go as planned and, if they do not, the necessary contingency plans to navigate what may be a difficult beginning.

Strategic planning usefully determines not only what will be done, but when it should be done. The initiation of a new phase of the incubator may or may not be made contingent upon the successful completion of an earlier phase. Can the operation begin as an "incubator without walls," providing business services before the facility is ready for occupancy? At what point in the development process is the manager hired? The notion that timing is everything is certainly true in strategic planning for an incubator spinout.

Outline clearly, three additional steps you would take to develop your business concept from an idea. Justify your response.

Lesson 4 - Entrepreneurship Resources

After taking this lesson you should be able to:

1. To identify what is needed to start the venture

2. To be aware of the available resources required for this venture

Introduction

The idea of resources usually leads us to think of only money. In this section, we will examine how to access the available resources and how to put it to work.

We will seek to answer the following questions:

1 How do we start a small business?

2 What do we need to start a business?

3 How do we access resources?

4 Is partnering to access resources a good idea?

Successful entrepreneurial processes require entrepreneurs and teams to mobilize a wide array of resources quickly and efficiently. All innovative and entrepreneurial ventures combine specific resources such as capital, talent, and know-how (e.g., Accountants, lawyers), equipment, and production facilities. Breaking down a venture's required resources into components can clarify what is needed and when it is needed. Although resource requirements change during the early growth stages of a venture, at each stage the entrepreneur should be clear about the priority resources that enable or inhibit moving to the next stage of growth. What kinds of resources are needed?

The following list provides guidance:

Capital. What financial resources, in what form (e.g., equity, debt, family loans, angel capital, venture capital), are needed at the first stage? This requires an understanding of cash flow needs, break-even time frames, and other details. Back-of-the-envelope estimates must be converted to pro forma income statements to understand financial needs.

Know-how. Record keeping and accounting and legal process and advice are essential resources that must be considered at the start of every venture. New ventures require legal incorporation, financial record keeping, and rudimentary systems. Resources to provide for these expenses must be built into the budget.

Facilities, equipment, and transport. Does the venture need office space, production facilities, special equipment, or transportation? At the early stage of analysis, ownership of these resources does not need to be determined. The resource requirement, however, must be identified. Arrangements for leasing or owning, vendor negotiations, truck or rail transport, or temporary rental solutions are all decision options depending on the product or service provided. However, to start and launch the venture, the resources must be articulated and preliminary costs attached to them.

Financial Resources

Finances are crucial, and the amount of money needed to start and run a business will depend on the type of product or service, the size of the business and many other factors.

Every start-up firm and young growing business needs capital/money to invest in growing the business. Some companies access capital from the company founders or the friends and family of the founders. Growing companies that are profitable may be able to turn to banks and traditional lending companies. Another increasingly visible and popular source of capital is venture capital. Venture capital (VC) refers to the investment made in an early- or growth-stage company. A venture capitalist (also known as VC) refers to the investor.

Sources of financing available to firms include foreign stock exchanges, foreign bond markets, foreign banks, venture capital firms, and funding from the parent company. Firms can also obtain funding via intra-firm loans or trade credits. A trade credit lets the customer (in this case, the subsidiary buying the goods or services) defers payment for the good or service for a specified period, typically thirty or ninety days. By borrowing capital from a parent company, both the subsidiary and the parent eliminate paying transaction costs to an outside entity such as a bank, which would charge fees to make the transaction.

Product/Service Concept

What are you selling? New ventures offer solutions to people's problems. This concept requires you to not only examine the item or service description but understand what your initial customers see themselves buying. A customer has a need to be met. He or she is hungry and needs food. Food solves the problem. Another customer faces the problem of transferring money electronically and needs an efficient solution, a service that satisfies the need. Automatic teller machines are developed, and services are offered. In any of these situations, in any entrepreneurial innovation circumstance in fact, as the entrepreneur you must ask the following questions:

- What is the solution for which you want someone to pay?
- Is it a service or product, or some combination?
- To whom are you selling it? Is the buyer the actual user? Who makes the purchase decision?
- What is the customer's problem and how does your service or product address it?

Understanding what you are selling is not as obvious as it might sound. When you sell an electric vehicle, you are not just selling transportation. The buyer is buying a package of attributes that might include cutting-edge technology, lower operating costs, and perhaps the satisfaction of being part of a solution to health, environmental, and energy security problems.116

Physical resources

The physical resources examine the resources concerned with the operation's ability to deliver its goods and services. These include manufacturing, marketing, production, and technology facilities for optimal operation. Appropriate physical resources are essential. This includes proper workstations, telecommunication systems, and marketing materials. The entrepreneur should properly evaluate the needs and wants before they begin operations.

Human Resources

People in companies provide skills, knowledge, intuition, and reasoning (known as human capital). Additionally, the culture inside an organization consists of relationships, values, and routines and companies that have a strong set of managerial values have a strategic advantage over those that don't- through employees increased identity with the corporation, increased stability, and consistency as well as a guide for appropriate behavior.

The human resource is the skill set of the business. To determine if the business has the desired skill set to ensure success the entrepreneur should;

1. Ascertain the number of staff required and qualification need to operate the business properly

2. Resolve the training needed to function in various posts within the business

3. Ensure that the working environment is conducive for the employees to function optimally

It is crucial that professionals be recruited with the relevant expertise to ensure that the objectives of the business are efficiently and competently done.

Internal environment

An organization evaluates which factors are its strengths and weaknesses; it is assessing its internal environment. Once companies determine their strengths, they can use those strengths to capitalize on opportunities and develop their competitive advantage. When organizations assess their internal environments, they must look at factors such as performance and costs as well as brand awareness and location. Managers need to examine both the past and current strategies of their firms and determine what strategies succeeded and which ones failed. This helps a company plan its future actions and improves the odds they will be successful.

External environment

Analyzing the external environment involves tracking conditions in the macro and the micro marketplace that, although largely uncontrollable, affect the way an organization does business. The macro-environment includes economic factors, demographic trends, cultural and social trends, political and legal regulations, technological changes, and the price and availability of natural resources. The microenvironment includes competition, suppliers, marketing intermediaries (retailers, wholesalers), the public, the company, and customers. Analyzing the environment becomes more complex because they must examine the external environment in each country in which they do business. Regulations, competitors, technological development, and the economy may be different in each country and will affect how firms do business.

There are several entrepreneurial development organizations that provide assistance to entrepreneurs to ensure the success of their venture. Refer to those in the country you are in right now as you are reading and studying.

Summary

There are different factors that impact the performance of any business venture. In this lesson, we examine the financial, physical, and human resources and their impact on business success. We also reviewed the internal and external environment for success. In the next lesson, we will investigate the implementation and management of business ventures.

Lesson 5 - Implementing and managing the venture

After taking this lesson you should be able to:

1. Develop an understanding of how to explain the activities involved in implementing and managing a venture.

Introduction

A business venture: is a start-up enterprise formed with the expectation and plan that a financial gain will result. This type of business normally starts out with an idea that begins with a small amount of capital or finances. Individuals consider a business venture or a small organization backed by one or more investors with the hope that the business will be profitable.

Business Concepts

We can note that a business venture results out of a need for something lacking or insufficient in the current market. Also, this need can be a service or product that consumers are requesting to satisfy a need or to serve a particular purpose. Therefore, once the need is recognized, an individual or investor that has the resources and time to develop and market the new commodity on the open market can start the venture.

At the start of a business venture, the investor should prepare a formal business plan to outline the purpose and mission of the business for the future. An effective business plan will include a quantifiable process for identifying additional finances, increasing gains and designing an escape plan should the business fail. One should note that many initial business undertakings fail within the first one to three years of inception. As a result, it is important to include a plan to liquefy the business if needed to reduce financial loss.

Entrepreneurs, often find easy coming up with a variety of ideas for new businesses and many difficulties to implement those concepts. Although the business concept is a bridge between an idea and a business plan, it directs the entrepreneur's thinking so that s/he can identify the specifics of his/her proposed venture. Transfiguring an idea into a business concept entails thinking about how the product or service will be sold and who will buy it, the values of the product or service, how it is distinguished from similar ones, and methods of delivery.

A clear business concept also allows the entrepreneur/founder to describe the specific nature of the business to suppliers, customers, lenders, and resource team members. When describing his/her business idea, the entrepreneur should answer the following questions:

a. What is my product/service?

b. What does my product/service do?

c. How is it different or better than other products/services?

d. Who will buy the product/service?

e. Why will they buy the product/service?

f. How will the product/service be promoted and sold/offered?

g. Who are my competitors?

Once the entrepreneur defines the business concept statement, the more detailed work of business planning and implementation may begin. You can conduct additional research using the World Wide Web to explore ways of starting business ventures as well as further insight on how to compose a good business plan. Also, you can gain knowledge from experts in your field of interest and across industries. There are many search engines to facilitate this exercise.

Monitoring Performance: The innovative entrepreneur sees the importance of monitoring the performance of the new business ideas to discover if s/he is delivering benefits. To accomplish this task, the entrepreneur must:

a. Set specific goals and targets: In most cases, new ideas or innovations originate to address specific needs or issues. Thus, they should either improve or enhance an existing product, process or service, or be completely new because of the research and development the entrepreneur has undertaken around a new trend or opportunity. Great investors make sure their targets are SMART - specific, measurable, achievable, realistic and time-bound.

b. Measure the performance of new ideas: No matter how the idea derived, it is essential to measure how well it is performing once implemented. The choice of doing this will depend on the nature of innovation and one's own organization. However, there are some simple calculations to facilitate the process, including:

• Research & Development expenditure as a percentage of revenue

• The cost of non-financial resources (including time and people)

• New product sales (less than 2 years) as a percentage of sales

• The percentage of profits from the new products/services

• The number of months to develop and launch a product (speed to market)

• Staff satisfaction and performance

• Customer feedback and satisfaction with your business.

c. Benchmark your business: the entrepreneur may find it useful to benchmark his/her business against other similar businesses in the industry or sector, to try to understand the impact and benefits of the innovation. Benchmarking against rivals could help the investor identify whether there are any goals and targets his/her competitors' use that could similarly benefit the business.

d. Act on goals and targets: When the goals and targets are achieved, the entrepreneur should consider additional or improved targets to help get the most out of his/her idea. However, when the goals and targets are not achieved, the entrepreneur should review and solve any specific issues which may be hampering the success, or consider whether his/her initial targets were unrealistic and should be revised.

The investor/entrepreneur should also explore the longer-term benefits of innovation, as well as the effect it can have in the short term. Since innovations can take the time to make a positive impact on your business operations, entrepreneurs are advised to include innovation as part of business planning. Having a business plan will help the entrepreneur to develop new ideas that meet the strategy and vision for the business.

Resources Provider

The definition of a provider is an individual person, organization or business that offers a good or service. Moreover, a resource provider is an individual, organization or business that offers services or goods to the entrepreneur for a successful venture. Starting a business can seem like an overwhelming task. In fact, it is. Research indicates many businesses that open each year, fail to last as long since there is no guarantee for success. An entrepreneur who has properly prepared may have an advantage in the competition.

In addition to a strong business plan, the entrepreneur should consider five resources that contribute to the success of a new enterprise:

a. Financial Resources: The most important element in starting a business is funding. Even the most basic business incurs several start-up costs, including registering a business name, obtaining a business telephone line and printing business cards. Financial resources can be obtained from multiple sources, the easiest being from the personal accounts of the business founder. Additionally, loans and lines of credit may be granted from financial institutions, friends and relatives, private investors and even the state government. Furthermore, many grants are offered from private and public sources to entrepreneurs/small business owners of all demographics and personal situations.

b. Human Resources: The success of an organization is profoundly dependent on the talent and strength of its employees.

The hiring of experienced professionals with records of excellence in their field of expertise safeguards that the mission and goals of the company will be executed and achieved. Strong team members can be recruited using several methods such as staffing agencies and executive search firms as well as referrals from individuals.

c. Educational Resources: Conceivably the paramount thing an entrepreneur can do when establishing a new business is to gain as much education possible. By understanding the competition and gaining an in-depth knowledge of the industry, s/he will be better prepared to make smarter decisions regarding the direction of the firm. Educational resources can be acquired through professional trade associations geared toward the industry, the local chamber of commerce as well as the Small Business Association and Administration.

d. Physical Resources: Whether a small business or a retail operation with multiple locations, every organization must have the appropriate physical resources to survive. This comprises a proper workspace, working telephone line, adequate information systems, and effective marketing materials. Since this aspect of business planning can be one of the costliest, it is important for an entrepreneur to assess his needs before making any purchases.

e. Emotional Resources: Starting a business venture can be a stressful undertaking for an entrepreneur. To maintain sanity as well as stay motivated, it is important that the entrepreneur has a support team that can provide inspirations and guidance as necessary. This team may entail friends and family as well as a mentor or professional group.

If your resource providers did not lay out repayment terms upfront, it is likely that they are "friends and family" rather than investors or venture capitalists. Consider ways in which you can create win-win for everyone involved in the success of the venture. The entrepreneur may consider fringe benefits and other offers for the human resources, negotiate loans and repayment terms conditions as well as offer shares in the business for major investors. Consulting with a professional consultant before making major decisions on paybacks to resource providers is advisable.

Reinvestment in the Business

Without a doubt, the most successful investors/entrepreneurs recognize the value of reinvesting at an early stage. When a business begins to generate profits, owners face two primary decisions: they can either distribute profits back to the owners or reinvest those profits back into the business to improve the company or expand operations. The decision of whether to reinvest profits or distribute them to the owners depends on several factors. However, there are some specific advantages to reinvesting profits.

- Reinvesting is the paramount way to build wealth.

- Reinvesting is crucial to your company's continued growth and success. Additionally, it is worth keeping in mind that investing is not just about a sudden inflow of cash; your time and experience is also valuable.

If you can apply your time, knowledge and experience in a way that profits your company in the long term, you will be making a valuable investment. Some form of reinvestment is necessary for any business to grow. It does not have to be all of the entrepreneur's profits, but a significant amount of resources, when effectively managed can dramatically increase your bottom line.

How to invest financially

The first thing that boggles the mind when one hears the word "reinvest" is a financial reinvestment. Redirecting a percentage of profits back into the business can help the firm grow and position itself for long-term success. However, the exact amount that you should reinvest will differ as the key is to reinvest based on a strategy, rather than a set percentage. Be strategic, and apply funds in line with your specific development plan and your business needs, but ensure there is enough to cover all of your other expenses.

One communal reinvestment is making business improvements. Hence, improving infrastructure, streamlining manufacturing, strengthening customer support, a refined marketing strategy can all directly benefit your business, increase your profits and reduce expenses, while giving you more capital to work with.

An investment in marketing will often pay off if the entrepreneur is smart with his/her marketing, and continually track the progress of the promotional initiatives. Therefore, when embarking on a marketing campaign, quantify the expected results to be able to monitor the success of the campaign.

It is important to invest in staff and build a resilient workforce. Taking care of one's employees will keep them happy as they will look forward to coming to work, and will be more loyal to the company.

How to know when you are ready to reinvest

Successful entrepreneurs made their wealth by investing wisely and not just as a one-time venture. In other words, it is a continual effort. Reallocating profits and other resources back into the business can help to establish the firm as a leading provider of the services or products offered. Reinvesting can also help to set the business on track for continued development.

Many people dislike reinvesting in their companies because they view it as spending money. However, investing is not about wasting money on superfluous expenses, it is about applying resources in a strategic manner that will result in increased profits and help you to achieve your long-term goals of continued growth and success.

How to invest expertise and experience

A sound strategy and good application of skills and knowledge are what will ultimately determine the success of any investment. Investing should always be done carefully, and with defined goals. It is about finding the best way to accelerate the venture forward and position the entrepreneur to be more profitable in the long term.

Training and education can also serve as an excellent investment. Training for self or your employees can pay off each time new skills are used. A well-educated workforce can be an important asset to the business, and smart firms invest in keeping their employees well trained and up to date on their credentials.

Finally, consider investing in a business coach or finding a mentor. Learning from others who have experience can often prove to be an invaluable investment. If you can gain support, time and assistance from others to improve your business, you will be significantly ahead.

Expansion of the business

The entrepreneur is the endless challenge seeker who recognizes that once the business is profitable, growth is the next exciting challenge. Exciting, but at the same time growth can make good business sense, such as better brand recognition, building value in the business for employees and customers, offering a wider range of products and services to a larger geographical market, and creating "economies of scale." As a result, rationalizing the rewards of a larger business could mean updating your business plan. The entrepreneur will need to update those spreadsheets, strategize the marketing plan and strategies an expansion implementation plan. Also, s/he will need to weigh the risks and rewards for growth.

Ways to Expand: From Local to Global

- Increase your sales and products in existing markets. This is the easiest and most risk-free way to expand. It may require a bigger location, different pricing strategies, as well as new/improved marketing techniques. However, it will be in a customer group with whom the entrepreneur already has a relationship.

- Introduce a New Product. You have a successful product/service that you have been offering for some time and have been gathering data, customer feedback and doing the fiddling on your newest product. This is a normal fruition in business, not just an expansion scheme. When placed as adding value and being responsive to customer needs, this can be a reasonably risk-free way to expand.

- Develop a New Market Segment or Move into New Geography. These areas require cost expenditures and doubt. Moving the products into new categories/demographic segments requires market research and new marketing strategies. This activity may absorb significant time and attention. However, while the risks are more, the payoffs are large. Therefore, for most businesses looking to expand, these two methods of expansion are inevitable.

- Start a Chain. A service business that is easily reproduced and can be run from a distance is suitable to launch a chain. However, the entrepreneur must be cognizant of what made the first location a success, i.e. was it the location, the staff or you? If it is just you, then replication is only possible through meticulous operations plans and sharing staff between locations. The entrepreneur will need to duplicate the plan of the first location while satisfying increased customer demands.

• Franchise / License. Although it is a quick way to grow, a franchise agreement can be costly to prepare. You will need to be a good teacher, be able to prepare the training manuals, be very organized and willing to travel. While licensing can carry less risk, it demands giving up a certain amount of control. Licensing a patent, trademark or industrial design means that you sell manufacturing, distribution or production rights.

• Join Forces / Strategic Alliance. A merger or acquisition combines two companies, expands your customer base, increases intellectual capital and delivers operational efficiencies. The hoax is locating the right partner.

• Go Global. The business owner can decide to go global in a number of ways. These may include but not limited to growing markets, rising consumer spending, or the improved business climate. In addition, sometimes the only place to find these things is overseas. Conducting international business can take the form of exporting, licensing, a joint venture or manufacturing, but whatever forms the entrepreneur chose, the basic business rules apply. These involve assess customer demand, gain legal and accounting assistance, protect intellectual property and obey regulations.

Achievement of performance goals

Performance management (PM) includes exercises that ensure the aims are consistently being met in an effective and efficient manner. In other words, performance management involves the way managers assess employees, how employees evaluate their managers and fellow employees, and how individual workers appraise themselves. The ultimate goal of performance management is to improve the quality of work in the most proficient manner possible. The performance management process is a means by which organizations align their resources, systems, and employees to strategic objectives and priorities.

Effective managers seek to provide feedback to and receive feedback from employees incessantly, rather than rely on infrequent appraisals. This allows a manager to determine what inspires employees to work hard, evaluate what impediments are making it difficult for employees to do their jobs effectively, and adjust employee workloads as necessary. Managers must identify which approach works best according to the situation and organizational culture. Managers have to ensure that employees are governed according to a company's policies, but must also ensure that cultural norms are taken into account.

Managing performance is essential to the relationship between managers and employees. It can be a key element of good communication and nurture the growth of trust and personal development. Managing performance is vital to how well your employees will be engaged in their work and how well they will complete given tasks. It is important to note that, an engaged employee is someone who:

• Takes pride in their job and shows loyalty towards their line manager, team or organization and

• Goes the extra mile – mainly in areas like customer service, or where employees need to be creative, responsive or adaptable.

Good performance management can contribute significantly to all drivers. Moreover, there are three aspects to planning an individual's performance, which include:

1. Objectives which the employee is expected to achieve

2. Competencies or behaviors – the way in which employees work towards their objectives.

Personal development – the development employees need in order to achieve objectives and realize their potential.

The 'SMART' acronym is a useful way of getting the objectives right. Objectives should be:

Specific – objectives should state the desired outcome. What does the employee need to achieve?

Measurable – How will you and the employee know when an objective has been achieved? How should employee performance be planned?

Achievable – is the objective something the employee is capable of achieving but also challenging?

Relevant – do objectives relate to those of the team/department/business?

Time-bound – when does the objective need to be achieved?

Summary

You just completed implementing and managing the venture in the entrepreneurial process. You have defined business venture, ways in which ideas can be generated for a business venture, monitoring of performance, resource providers, ways of paying back resource providers, reinvestment and ways the entrepreneur can reinvest in the business, benefits of reinvestments, ways in which the business can expand and achievement of performance goals in the business.

We will now look at harvesting the venture.

Lesson 6 - Harvesting the Venture

At the end of this lesson, you should be able to:

1. Assess the various options of harvesting a venture

2. Compare and contrast the existing strategies

Introduction

In this section, you will learn about the final step of the entrepreneurial process: harvesting the venture. The harvesting strategies include selling the venture, liquidation, mergers, and acquisitions. These options are used by entrepreneurs and investors when they seek to exit a business and recover their initial investment.

Reflection:

When is the right time to leave a business?

As an entrepreneur, do you plan to stop working one day? What will happen to your business?

Harvesting strategies include selling the venture, liquidation, mergers, and acquisitions. These options are used by entrepreneurs and investors when they seek to exit a business and recover their initial investment.

Harvesting options are:

Absorption of new concept into mainstream options:

This occurs when an area/activity of the venture is reduced or removed to recover funds to invest in a new concept or expansion of the product line. It is dependent on the financial feasibility of the project.

Licensing of Rights:

The entrepreneur may choose to sell the business rights. Permission is granted to an individual/company to manufacture, patent, copyright and trademark products using the licensing agreement. The agreement is legal and can be customized based on the access the licensors (entrepreneur) chooses to give the licensee.

Family Succession:

The entrepreneur/founder of the business may consider retirement or from being actively involved in the business and may choose a family member to be a successor.

Initially, family members can be given employment with the company. This provides the opportunity for the founder to mentor and guided participation of the successor in the business for a smooth transition when he takes over.

A written document succession plan should be created to address the new roles of management and structure of the organizations for all parties involved.

Go Public:

A business may decide to sell shares of stock to outside investors. Initial public offerings (IPO) exist when a company sells shares of its stocks to the public for the first time. The method is used to raise capital, however; it can be timely and expensive. Entrepreneurs may choose to go public to gain returns on initial investments. When this happens, a business chooses to sell stock to the public, the business status changes from private to public.

Employee Stock Ownership Plan (ESOP):

This involves an agreement with employees and managers to allocate a portion of their wages towards purchasing company stock from the founder until employees own the company.

Liquidate the Venture:

The entrepreneur may want to leave the venture and will liquidate assets, settle debts and severance employees. This exists when there are no prospective buyers.

Selling the Venture:

The owner may decide to sell the venture to an individual or company. Parties involved should agree on a sale price, transfer of ownership and other legalities of the business.

Mergers and Acquisitions:

An entrepreneur or corporate organization may decide to purchase the majority of all shares of another business. The organization may choose to merge as a strategy for expansion and growth.

Bert and Danny, two brothers, decided to form a partnership to open a dog kennel. They agreed Tony (Bert's son) would take over the business in 8 years. During the entrepreneurial process, Tony was mentored and guided to take over the business. After 8 years, the partners retired, and Tony was responsible for managing the kennel.

Harvesting the Venture

1. An entrepreneur may choose to fund an employee stock ownership plan: To exit the business

2. Placing a picture of Mickey Mouse to sell knapsacks is a form of: Brand licensing

3. Franchising is an advantage to the franchisor as: The franchisor gains revenue from fees and royalties

4. An initial public offering occurs: A private company offers a stock sale to the public

5. A management buyout results: The managers of the company take ownership

Summary

On completion of this lesson, you have learned about mergers, franchising and other harvesting options such as selling the venture, liquidation, and management buyout. An entrepreneur may harvest the venture not solely on the loss of profits, but for other reasons as a serial entrepreneur or retirement. You should be able to consider the most appropriate harvesting option for your business. You have now reached the last module of this course where you will learn about Creativity and Innovation!

Lesson 7 - Principles of Creativity

After taking this lesson you should be able to:

• Define creativity

• Explain the role and process of creativity in entrepreneurship

Introduction

This topic explores creativity in relations to entrepreneurial activities as well as the process of creativity within the workplace. In addition, the prominent entrepreneur(s) learn(s) the definition of creativity as well as, the roles of creativity, and the importance of creativity in business. We will begin by brainstorming and coining a definition of creativity. Moreover, the roles and importance of creativity in entrepreneurship that will broaden your knowledge and provide assistance for the analysis and interpretation of data shared.

Mrs. Thomas owns a mechanic store; her clients consistently demand her attention throughout the day. The tasks are vastly becoming uncontrollable for Mrs. Thomas to achieve within the short opening hours of operation. She discussed the problem with her son who provides assistance in the workplace twice per week. Amis is an innovative person who looked at the issues from a different perspective. He provided his mother with a solution that will allow her to accomplish her clients' tasks in a profitable way. If you were Mrs. Thomas' son, Amis, what are some of the solutions you would provide to solve the problem faced in the workplace?

Creativity Defined

Without a doubt, creativity does not just happen. In fact, the process entails the ability to envision situations in innovative ways, to discover unforeseen patterns, to make links between disparate phenomena, and to generate resolutions. Additionally, creativity involves two processes: thinking, a skill that can be developed and produced, a process that can and be managed.

In order to identify individual creativity, s/he must have a foundation of knowledge, mastery of thinking, display signs of exploration, and love to experiment, focus on discipline, question the status quo, use their imagination and synthesize information. In other words, the entrepreneur must be able to look at things in a complex approach from various perspectives. Additionally, s/he must learn to garner new ideas and think of alternatives that are unique. Therefore, the entrepreneur must be flexible, unpredictable with his/her tactics as well as tolerable of obscurities.

Think of a major project that you have organized in the past or one that you are presently organizing. Write down the steps you took in order to achieve success or the steps you have taken to get to the final stage.

The Creative Process

The creative process explains how an individual can form random thoughts into an ideal combination or solution. It is valuable to note that the basic five steps are important for creativity to be at its best.

- Preparation: During this step, an individual displays signs of curiosity after facing a problem. In addition, s/he may carry out research constructs objectives, organize thoughts and brainstorm the various ideas convey.

- Incubation: This step allows for the synthesizing of ideas through imagination and constructing of such ideas to facilitate creation.

- Illumination: This step allows the entrepreneur to be spontaneous as ideas can be obtained at the spur of the moment.

Although an individual may have an initial idea, several other ideas may generate as s/he continues to explore the concept and think outside the box. Illumination is that moment when the entrepreneur has an epiphany or unexpected brilliant idea.

- Evaluation: the brilliant idea may not be ready for execution so the entrepreneur must undergo an evaluation process to ensure that the pursuit is worth investing. In order to make a final decision, the entrepreneur may consult with other experts in the field to gain further insights.

- Implementation: Finally the entrepreneur can begin to transform his/her thoughts into a final product. This step is not set in stones and as such, the entrepreneur can begin to transform the idea or thoughts more than once until the desired outcome is achieved.

Process of creativity

Where creative ideas come from:

Roles and Importance of Creativity in Business

Undoubtedly creativity is important for any business venture. The act of creativity facilitates problem-solving by generating new innovative ideas that may further lead to success. Research has proven that the creative entrepreneur is happier in the long-run. This experience can be reflected in the workplace and serves as a motivation for others within the workplace. This can affect productivity within the business and lead to greater profitability. Creativity can drive progress within the business as it facilitates changes necessary to combat problems within the workplace.

Summary

You just completed principles of creativity. You have defined creativity, the process of creativity, roles of creativity and the importance of creativity in the business.

We will now look at the principles of innovation.

Lesson 8 - Principles of innovation

After taking this lesson you should be able to:

1. Define innovation
2. Explain the role and process of innovation in entrepreneurship
3. Discuss the types of innovation in relation to the 4Ps
4. List the core innovation concepts
5. Identify the sources of innovation

Introduction

Have you ever considered where good ideas come from? How new business ventures become a success? In this lesson, you will have an opportunity to examine the core concepts of innovations and the role and process of innovations in entrepreneurship.

Innovation is the creation of better or more effective products, processes, services, technologies, or ideas that are readily available to markets, governments, and society. Innovation differs from invention in that innovation refers to the use of better and, as a result, a novel idea or method, whereas invention refers more directly to the creation of the idea or method itself. Innovation differs from improvement in the innovation refers to the notion of doing something different rather than doing the same thing better.

Innovations are defined more narrowly as the ideas, the products, the services, and processes that (a) are perceived as being new and different and (b) have been designed, built, and commercialized. Innovation thus includes both creative idea generation and the actual implementation of the idea. An invention is an innovation that is not ready for prime time. Inventions are ideas that have been built or conceptualized, but not widely used and available and usually not commercialized.

The importance of Innovation

Innovation is an important driver leading to organizational

financial performance. It is after all the catalyst for developing differentiated products and services for competing in monopolistic competitive markets. Research and development are driven by the diffusion of science and the translation of basic science into commercially viable products and services. R&D by entrepreneurs may not involve basic scientific research, but it does involve searching for ideas that will lead to differentiated and marketable products and services.

Concept of Innovation

The concept of innovation implies that benefit is derived from applications of a new market or technological knowledge. Innovations are of practical use in providing new or improved products or services and/or enabling people and organizations to do things more effectively and/or efficiently.

It is perhaps appropriate here to stress the difference between product and process innovation. Product innovation relates to the development of a new product, for instance, a new piece of equipment such as the personal computer (PC). However, when an organization adopts this innovation to enable it to perform its operations more effectively and efficiently, it can be classed as a process of innovation. In effect, it is impacting on the process of the organization's activities. Keep in mind that what may be innovative for one organization may be 'old hat' for another.

Process innovation is not confined to the use of new equipment in an organization but, as Porter's definition of innovation suggests, can also refer to a new way of doing things. It is therefore important to remember that when we refer to technology in this course, we are defining it in its widest possible sense to include new equipment, machinery, and internet technologies, as well as new ways of organizing work, bound up in the systems, processes, and procedures of an organization and not necessarily involving physical equipment and products136.

When an innovative idea requires a better business model or radically redesigns the delivery of value of a focus on the customer, a real-world experimentation approach increases the chances of market success.

Sources of Innovation

There are several sources of innovation. According to the Peter F. Drucker, the general sources of innovations are different changes in industry structure, in market structure, in local and global demographics, in human perception, mood, and meaning, in the amount of already available scientific knowledge, etc. When an innovative idea requires a better business model or radically redesigns the delivery of value to focus on the customer, a real-world experimentation approach increases the chances of market success. Potentially, innovative business models and customer experiences can't be tested through traditional market research methods. Programs of organizational innovation are typically tightly linked to organizational goals and objectives, the business plan, and to competitive market positioning. One driver for innovative programs in corporations is to achieve growth objectives. Once innovation occurs, innovations may be spread from the innovator to other individuals and groups. This process can be described as using the "s-curve" or diffusion curve. This is known as the process of diffusion.

Summary

Innovation is the creation of better or more effective products, processes, services, technologies, or ideas that are readily available in markets, government, and societies. Innovation thus includes both creative ideas and the actual implementation of the idea. Innovation is essential for developing differentiated products, and services in a competitive business environment. The core innovation concepts are incremental, modular, discontinuous and architectural. Sources of innovation include new markets, new technologies, new political rules, limited options, changes in sentiments or behaviors, deregulations and changes in business models.

Reflection time: re-examine your product and/or service what creative or innovative strategy can you implement to advance your enterprise?

The next lesson will continue with Disruptive, Incremental,

and Open innovations.

Adapted from Entrepreneurship 10.1, (2012). Retrieved from https://www.oercommons.org/media/upload/authoring/6929/documents/Entrepreneurship10_1.pdf (CC BY SA)

(Source: Entrepreneurship Education for Secondary Schools, Teachers' Instructional Manual – MOE - Democratic Republic of Timor Leste

(Author unknown)

Adapted from WikiHow, (2016). Retrieved from http://www.wikihow.com/Come-Up-With-a-Business-Idea (CC BY NC)

Adapted from Wikipedia, (2016). Retrieved from https://en.wikipedia.org/wiki/Business_opportunity (CC BY SA)

Adapted from Entrepreneurship, Innovation, and Sustainable Business, (2012). Retrieved from http://2012books.lardbucket.org/books/sustainable-business-cases/s09-entrepreneurship-innovation-an.html (CC BY NC SA)

Adapted from Entrepreneurship, Innovation, and Sustainable Business, (2012). Retrieved from http://2012books.lardbucket.org/books/sustainable-business-cases/s09-entrepreneurship-innovation-an.html (CC BY NC SA)

Adapted from Challenges and Opportunities in International Business, (2012). Retrieved from http://2012books.lardbucket.org/pdfs/challenges-and-opportunities-in-international-business.pdf (CC BY NC SA)

Adapted from Wikipedia Retrieved from https://en.wikipedia.org/wiki/Disruptive_innovation (CC BY SA)

Adapted from Technology Innovation and Management Review, (2012). Retrieved from http://timreview.ca/article/520 (CC BY)

Adapted from Wikipedia, (2016). Retrieved from https://en.wikipedia.org/wiki/Social_entrepreneurship (CC BY SA)

Adapted from Wikipedia, (2016). Retrieved from https://en.wikipedia.org/wiki/Social_innovation (CC BY SA)

Adapted from Wikibooks, (2010). Retrieved from https://en.wikibooks.org/wiki/Getting_Started_as_an_Entrepreneur/Opportunity/Evaluate_Your_Idea (CC BY SA)

Adapted from Wikipedia. Retrieved from: https://en.wikipedia.org/wiki/Business_idea

Adapted from Saylor Academy, (2012). Retrieved from https://saylordotorg.github.io/text_sustainability-innovation-and-entrepreneurship/ (CC By NC SA)

Adapted from Saylor Academy, (2012). Retrieved from https://saylordotorg.github.io/text_international-business/s11-03-venture-capital-and-the-global.html (CC BY NC SA)

Listen https://www.youtube.com/watch?v=69n633cEcAQ (CC BY)

Adapted from Wikibooks, (2015). Retrieved from https://en.wikibooks.org/wiki/Management_Strategy/Analyzing_Resources_and_Capabilities (CC BY SA)

Adapted from Marketing Principles, (2012). Retrieved from http://2012books.lardbucket.org/books/marketing-principles-v2.0/s05-02-components-of-the-strategic-pl.html (CC BY NC SA)

Implementing and managing the venture by Renee Morris-Phillip is licensed under a Creative Commons Attribution-NonCommercial 4.0 International License.

Harvesting the Venture by Janelle O'Mard is licensed under a Creative Commons Attribution 4.0 International License. (CC BY)

https://www.youtube.com/watch?v=U7nEgYOcb5c (CC-BY)

Adapted from the Saylor Foundation, (n.d). Retrieved from http://www.oercommons.org/courses/developing-new-products-and-services/view (CC BY NC SA)

Adapted from Open Learn, (2016). Retrieved from http://www.open.edu/openlearn/money-management/management/technology-management/the-concept-innovation/content-section-1 (CC BY NC SA)

Adapted from Boundless, (2016). Retrieved from https://www.boundless.com/sociology/textbooks/boundless-sociology-textbook/education-13/the-functionalist-perspective-on-education-100/innovation-564-10335/ (CC BY SA)

DISCLAIMER

Disclaimer All the material contained in this book is provided for educational and informational purposes only. No responsibility can be taken for any results or outcomes resulting from the use of this material. While every attempt has been made to provide information that is both accurate and effective, the author does not assume any responsibility for the accuracy or use/misuse of this information.

www.ingramcontent.com/pod-product-compliance
Lightning Source LLC
Chambersburg PA
CBHW072028230526
45466CB00020B/1046